About the Author

Charles Marowitz has been directing plays professionally since he was seventeen. He has been artistic director of five different theatres: In-Stage in London, the London-Traverse, The Open Space in London, Texas Stage Company in Dallas/Fort Worth, and Malibu Stage in California. He was co-director with Peter Brook at the Royal Shakespeare Company Experimental Group and directed a number of West End productions, including Joe Orton's *Loot* (which won the Evening Standard Award for Best Play), *The Bellow Plays* by Saul Bellow, *Fanghorn* by David Pinner (with Glenda Jackson), *Fortune and Men's Eyes* by John Herbert, *Jump* by Larry Gelbart, *Crawling Arnold* by Jules Feiffer, and many more.

He has also mounted contemporary and classic productions in major theatres throughout Germany, France, Italy, and Scandinavia, his most recent being Vaclav Havel's *Temptation*, performed at Prague's National Theatre in the Czech Republic. His own play, *Sherlock's Last Case*, was presented on Broadway in 1989 with Frank Langella in the lead, and his free adaptations of Shakespeare, Marlowe, Ibsen, Strindberg, Feydeau, Moliere, Rostand, and so forth have appeared in volumes such as *The Marowitz Shakespeare* (Penguin Books), *Sex Wars* (Marion Boyars, Inc.), and *Boulevard Comedies* (Smith & Kraus).

He has over thirty books to his credit, most of which deal with acting and directing. His anthologies of theatre criticism include *Confessions of a Counterfeit Critic* (Methuen) and *Stage Dust* (Scarecrow Press). He has written regularly for publications such as the *Guardian*, the *London Times*, *LA Weekly*, the *New York Times*, and *American Theatre Magazine*, and taught acting and directing in a wide assortment of colleges and universities in Europe, the United States, and Canada. He is currently on the artistic directorate of Shakespeare's Globe on London's South Bank and a member of the Association of Literary Scholars and Critics.

<u>Also</u> <u>by</u> <u>Charles</u> <u>Marowitz</u>

Books and Collections:

The Other Chekhov
Essays Om Teater
Stage Dust
The Other Way
Alarums and Excursions
Recycling Shakespeare
Directing the Action
Burnt Bridges
Prospero's Staff
Potboilers
Clever Dick
Sex Wars
The Act Of Being
The Marowitz Shakespeare
Confessions of a Counterfeit Critic
The Method as Means

Plays and Translations:

Murdering Marlowe
Quack
Boulevard Comedies
Stage Fright
Bashville in Love
Sherlock's Last Case
Clever Dick
Wilde West
Disciples
Hedda
Artaud at Rodez
The Shrew
Measure for Measure
An Othello
A Macbeth
Variations on the Merchant of Venice
The Critic as Artist
The Marowitz Hamlet and Tragical History of Dr. Faustus
Cyrano de Bergerac
Makbett
And They Put Handcuffs on the Flowers

How to Stage a Play, Make a Fortune, Win a Tony, and Become a Theatrical Icon

How to Stage a Play, Make a Fortune, Win a Tony, and Become a Theatrical Icon

Charles Marowitz

LIMELIGHT EDITIONS

Published in 2005 by
  Limelight Editions (an imprint of Amadeus Press, LLC)
  512 Newark Pompton Turnpike
  Pompton Plains, New Jersey 07444, USA

For sales, please contact
  Limelight Editions
  c/o Hal Leonard Corp.
  7777 West Bluemound Road
  Milwaukee, Wisconsin 53213, USA
  Tel. 800-637-2852
  Fax 414-774-3259

Website: www.limelighteditions.com

Book design by Lisa A. Jones

Illustrations by Cliff Mott

Printed in the United States of America

LIBRARY OF CONGRESS CATALOGING-IN-PUBLICATION DATA

Marowitz, Charles.
    How to stage a play, make a fortune, win a Tony,
and become a theatrical icon / Charles Marowitz.--
1st Limelight ed.
        p. cm.
    Includes bibliographical references.
    ISBN 0-87910-322-1 (pbk.)
    1. Theater--Production and direction. I. Title.

PN2053.M359 2005
792.02'33--dc22
                                    2005019561

Contents

Introduction

There are many learned treatises on the subject of stage direction.

This isn't one of them!

Here, the object is to explain as clearly as possible how a play mediates from the page to the stage through a process supervised, in the main, by the efforts and ideas of a director. I deliberately employ the phrase "in the main," because it is common knowledge that theatre is a collaborative art and, inescapably, a compound of creative energies dispensed by actors, writers, designers, dramaturges, producers, agents, and critics, all of whom leave some mark on a production—even if, as in the case of critics, it is after the fact. (A critique of a play becomes an inextricable feature of its identity, even when reversed by future critics who may hold very different opinions than those who first witnessed it.)

I am proceeding from the fairly conventional standpoint that it is the director who is the fulcrum of theatrical events, and this handbook is intended to describe—plainly and non-ideologically—what a director must do in bringing a play to life on stage. It recognizes but eschews other methods by which plays sometimes come into being—that is, improvised by actors working within a group or permanent company, proceeding from an aesthetic or political aim that is different from, and often at odds with, the conventional process by which a writer's work is assigned or appropriated by a single individual called a director. The latter could be defined as a person (usually willful, sometimes dictatorial) who puts his stamp on every aspect of the production and assembles a group of collaborators who accept the assumption that their work will be subordinated to the "vision" or "conception" of the person marshalling all their efforts.

But even then, there is no agreed-upon formula by which a production evolves, and every play collides with a different set of necessities. And so, even though this handbook presumes to be generic, one has to accept that there is no such thing as a "generic" piece of theatre. Every play is unique. Every rehearsal situation throws up its own demands and militates for or against certain modus operandi. That being the case, one could argue it is impossible to produce a handbook on "how to stage a play," but I believe most people practicing theatre will accept that there is a convention that has evolved over a period of some four centuries, and so as long as one allows for the deviations I have described, it should be possible to provide some basic guidelines as to how to proceed to mount a production.

If that premise is valid, the following pages should provide some guidance to people wanting to learn the ABCs of an art form that, in a sense, has no formal alphabet to help it construct sentences or impose grammar but is constantly subject to the vagaries of both improvisation and innovation. As directors often say to actors: If you can use it, use it! If you can't, discard it!

The original name of this book was *How to Stage a Play*, but it occurred to me that such a title would limit interest to only a handful of drama students at a few scattered colleges and universities, and as I cravenly wished to bag a larger readership with a greater assortment of ambitions, I cold-bloodedly decided to cast the net wider and appeal to that multitude who desperately crave fame and fortune and pursue theatre as a means of self-glorification rather than artistic mastery.

Having now confessed my contemptible commercial motive, I hope readers will forgive what I fully admit to be an unconscionable act of self-promotion. However, to mitigate the dastardliness of my offense, I feel it is only fair to add that by acquiring the knowledge and expertise to properly direct a play, it must follow—as the night the day—that such work *would* elicit glowing notices, inspire an avalanche of ticket sales, and bring fame, riches and iconic status.

In any case, that is my rationalization and I'm sticking to it.

How to Stage a Play, Make a Fortune, Win a Tony, and Become a Theatrical Icon

Choosing the Play

"Choosing the play" is already something of a false
start, because in most instances, a play is chosen
by a producer or a producing organization and
then assigned to a director. But just as often, a
director finds a new script, or an old one he wishes
to revive, and persuades some well-heeled management to back it with him at the helm.
Occasionally, a group of actors anxious to display
their talents will raise the money privately, rent a
theatre, and subsequently "rent" a director as well.
Directors should be wary about accepting these
kinds of projects, as they almost invariably have
some interpretative strings attached (an actress
who is dying to startle the world with her bulimic
version of Hedda or an overambitious youth des-
perate to foist his roller-skating Hamlet alongside
Olivier's, Gielgud's, and Branagh's), which only
become known once the production has set sail
and it is too late to do anything—except, perhaps,
jump ship.

But assuming this is a play you have yourself chosen, because you have a notion as to how it should be mounted and are eager to realize it, there are certain steps that should be taken. If it is a new play, it is sensible to circulate it among three or four literate friends to see whether they share your enthusiasm. If they do not, it is equally sensible to consider their objections. If these do not dissuade you and you believe the work has virtues that others have failed to recognize, proceed by all means. Some of the most successful productions have been of scripts that have been circulating for five, ten, sometimes fifteen years, the virtues of which no one previously recognized. If your gut instinct says, "This is worth doing," your gut instinct is probably your best guide in the matter.

If it is a revival of an established play, it makes sense to do some investigations as to when it was last revived, in what part of town, and whether successfully or unsuccessfully. If it had a healthy run, there is a good likelihood that people will not beat down the doors to see it again—unless, of course, you have such a startlingly new interpretation that it can be given a completely new gloss, guaranteeing an experience unlike the one previously bestowed.

Once you have eliminated good reasons for not abandoning your choice, there are certain steps you should take in regard to the script.

First of all, you should divide it into its respective parts. This is to say you should examine to see how it *divides itself* into its various parts, so that you have a clear notion of its literary structure. This done, there is nothing to prevent you from combining parts or deleting others and giving it a shape commensurate with your notion of what you wish to express through it. But before playing fast and loose with a play's actual structure, it makes good sense to recognize it for what it is. To be negligent in this matter is to discover, often in the middle or late stage of rehearsals, that you have been proceeding in a straight line, whereas the play is essentially curvaceous or nonlinear.

As with the interpretation of a classic work, you can proceed in any direction you like—so long as you recognize that it might be a divergence from what the playwright originally intended. The pitfall is being so obsessed with your *re*interpretation of the work that you never see the play in its pristine, original form. Many turkeys have been hatched due to the ego's insistence that what is in the director's mind is far superior to that which was originally in the playwright's. But as a hasty corollary to this warning, I have to add that a really new and fertilizing idea is precisely what an old, established classic is longing for—and if you are fortunate to have digested the original and belched up a masterpiece of your own, heave ho!

It is common, in the case of new plays, for directors to organize readings or workshops of the work in question. Occasionally this can provide some useful input on the material because it lets in outside light. But one always has to bear in mind that a reading is only the tip of a very deeply submerged iceberg—only one dimension of a three-dimensional object—and for that reason can be misleading. The same is true of workshops, which, because they are founded on the premise that the play in question still needs work, can encourage a process that transfigures the script with "improvements" and, ultimately, destroys what original value it may have once possessed. (Dramaturges are particularly hazardous during this process, as they too proceed from a premise: namely, that they know better than the author how to develop and improve his play, a supposition I have never known to be proven true.)

Let us assume that you have avoided all the above pitfalls and you have a notion of what you want to do with this script. It is important to safeguard it, for from the very first discussion of the play, long before the first rehearsal, you will be bombarded with other people's views of the given material. Occasionally these can be edifying; more often than not, they will be misleading or subversive to your original ideas. It is a general rule in the theatre that everyone fancies himself a critic or a play doctor and almost everyone will have a "bright idea" as to how a play can be improved. Flee from these as you would a squadron of Valkyries, for they are usually only the outpourings of essentially uncreative people who believe they have been blessed by the Muse, when in fact they have only been goosed by the devil.

"What do you mean...too old to play Juliet!!!"

Finding the Actors

Most major cities have periodicals that disseminate the news of a forthcoming production to casting agencies, usually through trade papers such as *Backstage* or *Show Business*. Cities such as New York and Los Angeles have *breakdown services*, informing agents about cast requirements, that do the same thing. Your announcement to these outlets would describe the nature of the show being readied and the roles you are intending to fill. Within a very short time, you will be deluged with photos and résumés of willing and available actors. Auditions will be arranged at some convenient location, and the first clatter of the "cattle call" will be set in motion.

The first hurdle in this arduous process is filtering through the applications—a procedure seriously complicated by the fact that agents rarely discriminate as to what is actually needed for a particular production and proceed on the assumption that if a Caucasian blonde with a Southern accent is required, it is a role that can just as readily be played by a Zambezi immigrant who has not yet mastered English.

The lack of scruples among agents and their lackadaisical attitude toward their own clients will be the first irritation. The second will be that when you finally meet the prospective performers, you will discover that they bear virtually no resemblance to their résumé photos, and often their list of credits is either inflated, imaginary, or both. What is useful in examining these submissions is to bypass the roles these actors have played and examine the directors who have previously employed them. This is a much surer guide to their efficiency than a long list of credits from out-of-the-way productions in faraway places. If reputable directors whose reputations are established have employed them in the past, there is a much greater likelihood that they will be worth your time. Assuming those credits are legitimate, it means others will have already discriminated in their favor.

Audition procedures vary considerably. Some directors, or casting directors, provide only *sides* (short excerpts) from which actors are expected to give "cold readings." Others, recognizing the futility of such practices, will provide scenes in advance of the audition that at the very least will give actors some semblance of the characters they are expected to portray and the context from which they spring. In the case of experienced actors with more established reputations, it is usual for them to receive the script in advance and indicate whether or not they have any interest in trying out for the project.

After a careful weeding-out process, a group of actors will be scheduled for auditions—either for readings of the prospective play or to perform monologues, modern or classic depending on the play's requirements. The applicants are usually informed that their monologues should be no longer than two or three minutes and that they should have at least two ready for presentation in the event that a second is requested. They are also warned against being overly chummy with casting directors, a) because auditions are usually kept to a very tight schedule, with each actor allotted only five or ten minutes of audition time, and b) because it gives the impression of being self-serving (i.e., buttering up prospective employers) and is frowned upon by the Powers That Be. Certain impetuous actors are so hysterical about maximizing the opportunity to present themselves that they don weird costumes, assume exuberant and unnatural personalities, or engage in other forms of bizarre behavior, on the assumption that this will make them more memorable to the management. These antics usually succeed only in providing some comic relief for hard-pressed directors and stage managers, and can often destroy actors' credibility so totally that their names find their way on to an unofficial blacklist of "Oddballs to Avoid in the Future."

Once the auditions commence, it is important for a director to know what he is looking for. This is not simply an actor who may have the "look" of the character he is trying to cast (as looks bear almost no relation to an actor's ability to deliver the emotional requisites of a performance). What the director *should* be looking for is someone capable of taking direction, someone who, over a period of some four or six weeks, can be molded into a character emanating from the joint imaginations of playwright and director. To discover whether this ability exists, it is fairly useless for an actor simply to don his audition mask and perform his "party piece"—the speech he has perfected and delivered countless times to his mirror, teachers, friends, and colleagues. That is a disservice to both the actor and the director. It behooves the director to test the actor's ability to set aside the actor's original choices and attempt to realize the new suggestions being put to him. If the actor's audition piece is made of marble rather than clay, he may find it impossible to assimilate directions that attempt to alter it. That tells a director a good deal more than the timbre of an actor's voice or the manner of his outward bearing. It gives him a clue as to whether the actor is intellectually facile enough to take an idea and convert it into behavior and characterization. If the actor fails that test—no matter how splendid his look—he is probably undirectable, and hiring an undirectable actor is like placing a nondriver behind the seat of a powerful racecar that never leaves the starting line.

Since the object of the brief encounter is to discover the essence of auditioning actors, it makes good sense to engage them in some brief discussion about their past or present engagements—not merely to unearth facts but to discern the contour of their minds and the tenor of their personalities. Do they have humor? Are they articulate or are they dim? Are they relaxed or uptight? Do they have literary inclinations? Are they "armored" or accessible? All of these personality traits—the useful and the troublesome—will emerge in rehearsals, and so it makes sense to discover them before actors are contracted, and the audition is the obvious place to conduct such investigations.

Since the goal behind a rehearsal period is the growth and development of actors within a collective framework, the ability to change and develop is what the director should be trying to unearth. Too often directors have "thrown away a pearl richer than all their tribe" by scanting auditions or refusing to penetrate beyond the superficies of an impersonal encounter.

Callbacks—two, three, or even more—are a good insurance policy against errors of judgment. Every time an actor is called back to audition or read for a role, some new aspect of his personality gets revealed. First impressions are strengthened or possibly reversed. It is also important for actors to be called back to read with other actors who have already been cast, to insure that the proper chemistry exists between them. If one actor is extensively involved with another during the course of the play, it is essential that both coalesce in that delicate exploratory period before contacts are signed. In the theatre, as in life, the way one person interacts with another affects both parties. One actor will bring out new colors and new possibilities in another; others will dampen or diminish them.

The director pairing up actors for his cast is essentially performing the role of a matchmaker, and to do this successfully, the "matchmaker" has to learn as much as can be learned about each party before the match is finalized.

It is one of the theatre's great truisms that casting represents 90 percent of the entire theatrical process. Although this is generally true, it fails to explain the abysmal failure of plays that are often buttressed with star names and unimpeachable talents.

There is something more central to success in the theatre than the torque of name performers, and that is the chemistry a director engenders during those weeks when he draws out the imagination of his players in the service of his script. Of course, this transformation is predicated on the assumption that imagination exists in the first place, and that brings us back to the casting process. The director, like the gold prospector, must intuit the presence of precious metal before he begins to drill. If his initial instincts are wrong, no amount of digging will unearth anything worthwhile. If his instincts are sound, there is no limit to the treasure trove that can be dredged from the depths.

Casting the Designers

The verb *casting* is used advisedly here, for designers need to be as carefully "cast" as actors.

Every able designer has a stylistic inclination of his own. Some are elaborate, others minimalist. Some, like certain dutiful actors, follow directions; others are prone to invent wild scenarios of their own that they then present to their director. If you are preparing an innovative reinterpretation of an Elizabethan or Jacobean classic, the workmanlike designer who is used to doors, walls, and living-room furniture will probably not serve your turn. If you are staging a two-act domestic comedy or drama, you may find the ideas of the overambitious designer too grandiose for your room-sized entertainment. Since you are trying to establish a meeting of the minds with your designer, to discover whether both of you are on the same wavelength, the best way to "audition" him is without recourse to drawings or sketches, simply probing his imagination along the lines of your own to see if both veer in the same direction. It is not commonly accepted that designers, apart from possessing visual and decorative skills, also possess intellect. In fact, it is the latter that gives the former their special tang. Being on the same wavelength involves opening up lines of verbal communication with a person to fathom the depth or shallowness of his mind. Once a director and designer can share the same basic approach toward the prospective production, they have reached a plateau where collaboration is possible.

But in most cases, designers haul out portfolios crammed with sketches and photos of past accomplishments, and the director nods approvingly as he turns the pages, looking for some indication that this designer may share a conception of a play that he himself has not yet formulated. The way to open a conversation with a designer is not to say: "What I see on the stage is...etc., etc," but rather: "What this play seems to me to be about is...etc., etc." If the director expresses a vision of his material, that is something a designer may either share or cringe from. Designs are the last things that should be on the agenda in those first conversations.

Of course, the same applies to costume designers—with the proviso that instead of discussing renderings or sketches, they should be discussing *clothes*. What kind of clothes would such-and-such a character, in such-and-such a situation, be wearing. Forget about the colors and the texture, the outline and the style. All of that can be decided later. Start with a verbalization of the notion of the play as you see it.

Some directors have rich, vivid imaginations and can visualize precisely what their characters should be wearing—right down to color combinations and texture of material. A designer is well advised to take these suggestions seriously, because they are the manifest tokens of the director's theatrical imagination. That doesn't mean they can't be improved upon or altered when a director "alteration finds." But often, a designer sees himself as stepping into the ring with a director so as to foist his own vision of the work against another, the tacit assumption being: "I am an artist as well as you, and I am entitled to my artistic expression in color and design, just as you are in regard to text and staging." But that mental stance assumes that a work of art is capable of assimilating two mutually exclusive conceptions of the same material, and although that may be feasible sequentially—"I do my show then you do yours"—it is virtually impossible within the context of the same production. In nine cases out of ten, a designer is obliged to accept, embellish, and perfect a visual conception that is born out of the director's instinctive view of the work in hand.

That doesn't exclude the possibility that a designer, tuned into the director's wavelength, cannot suggest a richer and more fascinating version of the director's brainchild. That is very often the case, and just as a flexible director should be prepared to relinquish his interpretation of a particular speech when an actor comes up with an obvious improvement on it, so he should be prepared to discard his original visual conception of a show when a designer comes up with something better. If there is aesthetic unanimity on the part of designer and director in regard to fundamentals, the degree of cooperation is limitless. But if that unanimity does not exist from the outset, it can be as destructive as marital incompatibility and often ends the same way.

There are some star designers who are eminent enough to adopt a take-it-or-leave-it attitude to a project. There is one such (who will remain nameless) who, after reading a script, concocts the design he is prepared to deliver if hired and clearly presents it to the director. If the director disapproves or requires changes, the designer simply declines the project and suggests that the management find a more pliable collaborator.

This imperious attitude inspires a good deal of awe among many in the profession but is, in fact, a form of extreme egocentricity. It implies that his conception of a play may brook no disagreement with either the director's or the playwright's, and awesome as this attitude may be, it is an intransigence that has lost him several first-class productions, simply because he refused to be second-guessed by *anyone*—not even the director who comes with his own interpretation or the playwright who should certainly have a right to express an opinion about the work he has sired. There are instances in the theatre when the star of the show is not the director, playwright, or leading player but a charismatic and much sought-after designer, and when final authority is vested in such a person, the natural chain of command has already been subverted, and one should be prepared for lopsided reviews.

In the American theatre, set and costume design are irrational. Before the director and his company have discovered the nature of the characters, the meaning of their situations, and the point of the play, the costumes are completed and the sets ready to be shipped from workshop to the theatre. That is an imperative that the theatre places upon itself because it takes a goodly amount of time to build costumes and construct sets. But as I say, it is irrational. For an actor in the final stages of his rehearsal may suddenly discover the true nature of his character and find that he wouldn't possibly wear a costume like the one the designer, without reference to the actor's creative process, has created for him. The same holds true for sets that are preconceived before rehearsals are begun and usually cannot be changed in the event that the director and the actors (and sometimes even the playwright) come to the conclusion that the physical ambiance of the characters' world requires something very different.

To avoid fatalities of this kind, it is best to defer costume and set decisions to the very last moment—despite the outrage it creates among cutters and workshops—in the hope that their artistic legitimacy can be confirmed as the rehearsals draw to a close. People who militantly observe schedules and are obsessed with bureaucratic efficiency will throw up their hands in horror at such dilatory behavior, but the benefits, if any, will accrue to the production. There is such a thing as being "bang on schedule" and *wrong*, as opposed to being tardy and causing havoc but *right*. The clock is the tyrant of all artists in the theatre, and it may be high time that it was overthrown.

"When I said once more with feeling, I didn't mean..."

Reading the Play

It has become the custom, particularly in avant-garde companies and unorthodox productions, to replace a first reading with improvisations or exercises in some way related to the underbelly of the work about to be undertaken. Joan Littlewood began work on Brendan Behan's *The Hostage* with the actors being marched around the roof of their theatre in London's East End, trying to inculcate the kind of regimentation that many of its characters would have experienced in their military careers. Several companies find it useful to perform a series of sound-and-movement exercises as a preamble to rehearsals, in order to loosen up actors and get them to interact with each other without the constrictions that a text will shortly impose.

But these are the exceptions. In most cases, the first day is devoted to the first read-through of the play, either with or without the presence of the playwright, depending on circumstances. It is a day usually charged with tension, as actors feel they have to justify the fact that they have been hired and, consequently, try to prove themselves to their fellow actors. Or contrariwise, some actors (usually of the Method persuasion) will deliberately underplay their roles, clearly indicating that since no firm decisions about interpretation have yet been made, they refuse to assert feelings or attitudes about which they are not yet certain.

At the first read-through of Peter Brook's production of *King Lear* at Stratford-upon-Avon, starring Paul Scofield, the company began reading listlessly and without much purport, but when Scofield went at the text hell-for-leather, the other actors all took his lead and gave a spirited rendition of the play. Scofield wanted publicly to "test" the words he had been studying for many weeks in private and so dove in. Because of the high respect in which he was held by the other members of the company, they felt honor-bound to join him.

The degree of intensity conveyed during a first read-through is very much an individual matter, unless the director cues the tenor of the reading toward either quiet reflection or full-blooded histrionics. A spirited and "all out" reading has several advantages to a subdued or inaudible mouthing of the entire text. It gives the company a chance to experience the shape and sound of the material at hand—which private study before rehearsals cannot provide. It can also be used by the director as a barometer to test the preconceptions actors have of their roles. Often the root of a characterization problem is immediately revealed in the first reading. One sees in the blink of an eye an actor's misconception, a deeply rooted faux pax which is taking him in the wrong direction, and it signals the remedial action that will have to be undertaken once rehearsals begin in earnest. The great disadvantage of an all-out first reading is that an actor succumbs to his initial interpretation of the role, and the ultimate performance, after weeks of rehearsal, is little more than a gloss on the rendering he gave when he first sat with script in hand. That is a good argument for a slow, gradual, and uncertain start: a cautious crawl before the actor feels able to walk upright.

Certain directors believe the first rehearsal should also be something of a seminar on the play, with hefty analyses of the writer's intentions and articulated insights about the play's intellectual content, social milieu, and psychological subtext. If the playwright is present, that tendency is more likely to hold sway. Even directors, in the presence of authors, feel the need to prove themselves, exhibit their intellectual credentials, and articulate their beliefs. It is sometimes useful to hear playwrights speak openly about their plays, just to see what seems to be important to *them*. But in my experience, most playwrights shy away from declarations of intent. They know what they have written and why it has taken the shape it has, and rather than incline actors to their version of the material, they prefer to let the play speak to the actors in its own voice to see what will organically evolve. Playwrights such as Samuel Beckett and Harold Pinter flatly refused to discuss the rationale of their work in any terms and relied almost entirely on the impetus of the material on the talents of their players. That is a sensible policy, as it puts the onus on actors to find their own way, draw their own conclusions, and exercise their own imaginations.

In the earliest stage of my production of Vaclav Havel's *Temptation* at the National Theatre in Prague, the playwright spoke only of the circumstances under which the play was written, its gestation period while he was incarcerated by the Communist regime. He also described how he was gradually seduced by the idea of diabolism, which came from his reading of Thomas Mann's *Doctor Faustus*, Goethe's *Faust*, and Marlowe's *Tragical History of Doctor Faustus*. Nothing explicit was ever spoken about the meaning of the play or its author's intentions, but the details of its progeny cast a palpable spell on the company and unconsciously directed its thoughts to the issues underlying Havel's work.

If the actor's job is to discover the subtext that gives life to the text of his play, the more he probes its spiritual and philosophic roots, the greater his eventual discoveries will be.

Punctuation

A play is like a sentence consisting of both words and actions, and like a sentence, it needs to be correctly conjugated and contain correct grammar and syntax. Most importantly, it needs to be properly punctuated.

When a sentence is properly punctuated, its commas, colons, hyphens, parentheses, and periods help make it comprehensible and impose an appropriate rhythm. The same holds true for a play.

On stage, a comma may divide one thought from another, or it may distinguish the end of one mood and the start of another. On stage, an indentation denotes the start of a new unit, signaling the end of one *beat* (or section of emotional content) from the one that follows. A period (i.e., a full stop) may denote the conclusion of one objective and the commencement of another. An exclamation point may be used for emphasis on stage, in precisely the same way it is used in writing. The absence of punctuation will suggest a continuum of thought or an unbroken succession of thoughts over a fairly long period of time (i.e., a lengthy speech, a monologue, or an extended stretch of dialogue.)

Not only must the actor's text be punctuated for clarity and precision, but the scenes that make up each act need to be shaped for maximal effect—just as one would shape a series of paragraphs written to be read.

On stage, a lack of dramatic punctuation can be damaging to the narrative line of the play. It may blur meaning and combine things that are intended to be separated. It may elongate a tempo that needs to be accelerated or retarded, fragmented or integrated. If in the first scene of *Hamlet*, Francisco and Barnardo's text is not broken up with the tensions attendant on their guard duty, the arrival of the Ghost will be neither frightening nor suspenseful. If in the first "Court" scene, Hamlet's asides are not played in a different tonality from those of Claudius, Gertrude, and Polonius, his attitude to both his parents and his life at the court will be unclear. In the first soliloquy—which begins "O that this too too solid flesh would melt"—if the disjointedness of Hamlet's thought, its interruptions and sudden stops and reversals, are not clearly punctuated, we will not get the full impact of the character's inner turmoil, the moral confusions that are swirling around in his head. Proper punctuation on stage, as in writing, is an invaluable tool for clarity, and virtually every moment of rehearsal is concerned with clarifying insights that actors and directors have discovered in the play. The quest in rehearsals is always to *find meaning* and then make it *meaningful*, and dramatic punctuation is the means by which meaning is pried out of the text.

Let me switch metaphors.

A play is like a piece of music, the tonality of which is determined by changing key signatures and applying different dynamics. Speeches, scenes, units, and beats can often be characterized by descriptive musical terms: *largo, presto, allegro, allegretto, forte, fortissimo, piano, pianissimo, andante cantabile, sforzando, rallentando,* and so forth: all of these musical terms have dramatic corollaries. The start of the "Balcony" scene in *Romeo and Juliet,* because it is taking place at night in hazardous circumstances, may begin largo and pianissimo, although as soon as Romeo reveals himself to Juliet, it becomes forte and presto. When the danger attendant on Romeo's rash visit has been put aside by the mutual affections expressed between the would-be lovers, the offstage voice of the Nurse calling Juliet back into her bedroom may introduce a sforzando, which leads to a spirited and somewhat agitated allegro. The scene is as much about fear as it is love, and when emotions such as fear and love are intertwined on stage, one has almost entered a kind of operatic convention, and musical terms are not all that alien to describing what is taking place.

Dynamics and punctuation are ways of creating variety in dramatic material, and the instinct to vary what actors are doing is a constant factor in rehearsals. The fear is always monotony or not finding those changes inherent in a script that usually denote related changes in the subtext. The director is always using his personal mine-sweeper to discover what is lurking beneath the surface of the text, and the actor is always trying to divine what a character is *really* feeling as opposed to what he is saying. Once those discoveries are made, they need to be translated into rhythms and tonalities, pauses and continuums, highs and lows. Once those discoveries are made, they need, via punctuation, to be grooved into the mise-en-scène.

It is important to realize that a script, despite containing conventional grammar and syntax, does not arrive, theatrically speaking, "punctuated." It is the director in conjunction with his actors who are obliged to turn its words into actions; its actions into units; its units into tempi; its lines into "throughlines." An unpunctuated play is like the ingredients of a stew thrown into a pot but never cooked.

"It's marvellous—but it could stand a snip
here and there."

Settling for Less

Every director occasionally makes mistakes, and the most common errors are in the area of casting. It often happens that in the middle of a rehearsal process, a director finds that the actor in a key role simply cannot cut it. What is required of him cannot be delivered because it simply does not exist. You made a mistake. You were misled by an exceptional audition or persuaded by other people's opinions and therefore ignored that small, niggling inner voice that was sending out alarms, and now you are paying the price.

The most expedient remedy is to remove the person that's posing the problem. Replacement. It is often the course that seems the most extreme, because (a) it may disturb the morale of other members of the company, and (b) it seems a little heartless to punish another for what, essentially, is your mistake. But if all else has failed, replacement is the most practical course—assuming, of course, you can find a new actor who can actually deliver the goods.

But at such times, when the director is suffering an anguish that rarely conveys itself to his company but is no less intense for being suppressed, another impulse rears its ugly head: the impulse to "settle for less." The actor can't deliver what this role requires, so I will quietly compromise and come to terms with the inadequacy of the situation. This is like ignoring an x-ray that clearly indicates you have a tumor. The problem will grow and fester and reach a point where the only way you will be able to bear the inadequate actor is by refusing to acknowledge his presence. But the other members of the company and subsequently the audience will be less inclined to settle for less. They will receive the full brunt of the problem you tried to sweep under the carpet and, whether they recognize it or not, will react negatively to what they see and hear.

What, then, are the choices? The most obvious are either fire the artist or retain him and accept the harm he inflicts on your show.

There is a third way, however, and it is the hardest of all—hard on the actor as well as the director. It consists of openly acknowledging the actor's insufficiency and refusing to let it fester and infect the surrounding context. It involves

direct confrontation and brutal honesty, an unqual-
ified acknowledgement of precisely what is lack-
ing in the actor's performance and a joint resolve
to try to supply it: a process that is equivalent to
entering intensive care.

This involves stripping away the accumulated
traits, readings, inflections, and conceptions that
have been assiduously built up over the rehearsal
period. Going back to square one. Abandoning the
text and employing improvisation, a variety of acting exercises, and in-depth maneuvers to
"unblock" the actor and cause him actively to
rethink everything he has been doing from the very
first reading. It also involves a certain humility on
the part of the director: acknowledging that he too
has been wrong in allowing certain tendencies to
develop that have led only into a cul-de-sac.
Together, the director and the actor drill past the
text and the subtext to that amorphous area below
where theatrical gestation begins.

The nature of the exercises and the subjects
of the improvs will always be directly related to
the specifics of the problem being tackled, and it is
best for this work to be done only between the
actor, the director, and those one or two characters with whom the performer regularly interacts.

It should not be a "company project" conspicuously carried out before all the members of the cast. On the contrary, it can only work if it becomes the subject of intense private explorations between the problem actor, his immediate playing partners, and the director.

It is a painful process, because it is predicated on the belief that there is something terribly wrong and drastic measures have to be employed to correct the situation. But as with a behavioral problem thrust into the hands of a benevolent psychoanalyst, a measure of good will has to exist on both sides. The process is not a punishment but an extreme remedy in order to effect a dramatic change where one is desperately required. It is time-consuming and laborious; it can be injurious to the nervous system and can go terribly wrong if a breakthrough is not effected. But when it works, it can not only salvage the actor's performance but improve the overall texture of the entire production.

In a production of *Othello*, I was confronted with such a problem in regard to the actor playing the lead role. He was a black actor with a strong voice and a powerful presence, but in all of his scenes, he projected a suave and unruffled facade—even when he was being diabolically manipulated by Iago or cruelly contemptuous of an allegedly faithless Desdemona. It was as if he was afraid to reveal the fire that was burning inside of his character or unleash the ferocity that had been stirred up by Iago's provocations. Perhaps I had made a wrong casting choice, had been duped by the actor's natural attributes: his resonant bass voice and strong physical presence. But I refused to admit that was the case. The actor seemed to have all the attributes needed for the role, and there was something either he or I was doing that was preventing the emergence of the character.

We went into private sessions. I was deliberately provocative: I created harsh, even humiliating exercises that forced him to react strongly, and little by little, he took the bait. We segued from improvs back toward the Shakespearean text. Iago, with specific instructions from myself that had nothing to do with the logic or truthfulness of the scenes, also goaded and provoked the actor into aggressive behavior—so much so that on one occasion, I had to break up a heated scuffle. After an arduous eight or ten sessions, something was loosed in the actor that could be transferred to the character. Rehearsals progressed rapidly to the preview stage. Everyone in the company, who had been tacitly as worried as myself, breathed a sigh of relief. The actor had "found his role." Othello had arrived.

In this case, it turned out that deep within the actor's psyche there was the fear that if he showed the cruel and vicious aspects of a black character too blatantly, it would in some way reinforce the prejudice that many people felt toward blacks, and so unconsciously he was pulling all his punches. Had I been an analyst, I might have confronted the actor with the nature of this block, and we could have discussed it openly. But since I was a director and he an actor, the symptoms of the problem had to be routed out without direct reference to their cause. It didn't matter. The arduous extra sessions managed to unlock what the actor himself had placed in a tight, firmly locked compartment. I suppose that in the early, dark days of those rehearsals, I might have settled for less, but that would have meant countenancing an interpretation that was at odds with the playwright's intentions, and I felt that was unconscionable. But I have to admit that in other, similar circumstances, I lamely accepted inadequacies that there was simply no time to remedy, and I did settle for less.

Those are the sins of omission that a director never forgets or ever forgives.

Director and Playwright at Work.

Talking to Actors

Everyone has a language of his own, even if ostensibly we are all speaking English. Class differences, where we were born, where we were raised, what intellectual stimuli we received or didn't receive—all of these factors make up the language we speak. On some level of social intercourse, we all understand each other, but that doesn't alter the fact that each person's idiom differs from another's. A boy brought up in the rough-and-tumble atmosphere of a ghetto will possess a frame of reference very different from that of a boy brought up in a British public school. Their languages will reflect their differing social orientations; comprehension of certain words will ring differently in their respective ears. Just as everyone has his own penmanship and set of fingerprints, we all have our own personal glossary, and in the theatre, where communication between director and cast is the quintessential creative tool, it is important to find the language peculiar to each actor in order to be properly understood.

If, for instance, you are working with actors who are intelligent and well read and think conceptually, you can make reference to philosophical or psychoanalytical terms and quite probably they will grasp your meaning and your suggestions will bear fruit. But if you are working with an actor whose education stopped at junior high school—whose vernacular is simple, unadorned, and basic—those same terms will be not only confusing but irritating as well.

What is the portent of a "direction" anyway? Here is Glenda Jackson on the subject in a conversation from my book *Prospero's Staff*, referring to work with John Barton, Michel St. Denis, and Peter Brook at the Royal Shakespeare Company:

> If a director comes as Barton and St. Denis did, with everything taped, very clear on specifics and how each scene should be expressed, what is never there, in that kind of work situation, is the real energy of the scene. Which is very different from somebody like Peter Brook, who may have no idea at all about the specifics but is absolutely clear on the *kind* of energy that each scene has to pour into an auditorium. He may simply say: "Well, it's just on too small a level. It's very nice but that's not really what the scene is about. The scene is about a clash of titanic forces." Well, if somebody says

to you "clash of titanic forces," you already have to look and think in a different way, and what you then find to express, *that* is always exciting and interesting and invariably organic. Whereas if somebody says, oh, you know, "He gives her the letter" or "She kisses his hand" or something, and simply gives you a number of specific actions to perform, I find that utterly demoralizing.

In the instance cited, Brook found a direct path to Jackson's imagination. He used verbal imagery that gave her a kick-start into a general direction, which enabled her to find relevant particulars. Knowing Brook, I am aware that there are other actors with whom he would employ much simpler terms, words more closely approximating "specific actions to perform," and they would be happily accepted by these performers because easily understood.

With some actors, it is useful to find terms that are specific to their particular frames of reference, once you discover what they are. I once had an actor who was an old cinema buff, and when I told him that the scene needed "more of a touch of the George Zuccos," he knew precisely what I meant. Another actor was a car enthusiast, and when I suggested that a speech needed to be "nitrous oxidized," he immediately leapt on the suggestion and charged up his interpretation. I am not suggesting that a director needs to acquire the full vernacular of each and every actor. In most cases, basic English does the trick, but if one is trying for a nuance or something that has to be dredged up from a much greater depth, finding precisely the right words is like finding precisely the right key to open a chest or precisely the right power tool to get a carpentry job efficiently done.

The other point alluded to by Glenda Jackson is that a suggestion directed to the imagination can be much more effective than giving actors specific physical tasks to perform. Specificity of that kind speaks only to the actor's motor actions, whereas a stimulating or provocative suggestion couched in a vivid simile or metaphor may activate creative buds that lie beyond signal reactions. Of course, an excess of the latter can easily generate semantic confusion, and if a director is too fancy, it not only confuses actors but angers them as well. The great Russian actress and teacher Maria Ouspenskaya, an alumnus of the Moscow Arts Theatre, once asked an acting student to try to "be" a chocolate malted. He tried with all his might to create the essence of chocolate maltedness in his voice and body. When he was finished, Ouspenskaya shook her head and said, in her Slavic-lilted English: "No, you vass vanilla!" Directorial distinctions of that kind can drive actors to drink—or worse, into TV soap operas.

The other point about direction is that it shouldn't be *indirection*. If a director, out of courtesy, timidity, or fear of giving offence, or a thousand other lame rationalizations, pulls his punches, he will only exacerbate his problems. Obviously one shouldn't be insulting or contemptuous, but one should be *direct*, choosing precisely the right adjectives and adverbs to describe what is being presented by the actor and what is being sought. Some directors are blunt; others equivocate. The blunt ones can ruffle feathers, because all actors have egos and no one likes to be found wanting. But acting is a profession for adults, and if actors are hypersensitive to criticism, they are in the wrong business. Equivocating, finding weaker words to convey strong objections, does a disservice to both actor and director. A good actor will respect honest criticism frankly expressed; a hypersensitive actor may take umbrage, but nine times out of ten, the former actor's performance will be improved and the offended actor will come around. If one wants to achieve honest results, honesty among colleagues is unquestionably the best policy.

Rhythm and Tempo

The director has a lot of responsibilities. He has to monitor the work of the set, light, and sound designers. He is responsible for the production's continuity and clarity. He has to insure that language is comprehensible and audible. He must uproot, verify, and convey the play's subtext. He must oversee the schedule of rehearsals so a proper amount of time is spent excavating and analyzing, leaving sufficient time for drill before battening down the hatches. But one of his most important responsibilities is generating and maintaining a show's rhythm and tempo.

Rhythm refers to the "key signature" of each individual scene, and *tempo* encompasses the overall pacing of the show from start to finish. Some scenes are written to be played in 2/2 time, some in 2/4, some in 6/8, and so forth. Of course I am not referring to strict metronomic time, but there is a rhythm that pulses under every scene, and the director has to determine what rate of speed is most appropriate for it. Tempo is rooted in the links that exist between cues and scenes and the sequence that regulates the transitions between changing atmospheres. When we say a play "dragged," we are almost always criticizing rhythm and tempo.

Performances can be played too quickly, but the more common fault is that they are too slow. When unnecessary gaps exist between one speech and another or one scene and another, this is usually because actors are not picking up cues quickly enough. Some directors will deliberately retard the rhythm of a scene in order to insure that certain important information "gets through" to the audience, but this is almost always counterproductive. The point to bear in mind is that there is nothing faster than the speed of thought, and our minds have been hardwired to assimilate rapid-fire exchanges of dialogue and complex stretches of monologue, all of which communicate so long as diction and intention are clear. Speed with definition is always comprehensible, no matter how fast the tempo.

Tempo without definition is always incomprehensible. Tempo is a constituent of language. When we speak quickly, our physiology is conveying excitement or enthusiasm, anxiety, or apprehension. When we speak slowly, we are often conveying deliberation and reflection, tenderness, or fatigue. The emotional qualities of those words are inextricable from the rhythm in which they are couched, which is why an actor has to determine their frequency as well as their meaning. Indeed, their frequency is part and parcel of their meaning.

Often, a rapid rate of delivery is preliminary to a pause, and the preceding rhythm is what gives the pause its power. Sometimes a fast stretch of dialogue precedes an unexpected physical action or a contrasting rhythm: a slow verbal wind-down. These segments need to be composed the way a composer arranges the dynamics of a musical score: employing variety not for variety's sake but because language and intention normally expressed are constantly changing according to the flow of emotion that runs beneath every intention, every human mood, every psychological transition.

In a musical rehearsal, the orchestra conductor shapes the changing pattern of the composer's score according to his conception of the music. When the concert is given, those predetermined choices constitute his interpretation. The director is going through the same process when he posits a slow rhythm after a fast one, a staccato after a legato, tumult after calm, levity after gravity. The resultant variety, if it all works, captures and expresses the endless variety of human intercourse. When it drags or is boring, seems reiterative or redundant, it usually means the director has not done his job.

Esprit de Corps

Esprit de corps is a military term that refers to the "spirit of the company" and is predicated on the assumption that in order for a congregation of soldiers to operate efficiently and effectively, it is necessary for them to be inspired with pride in their collective identity and proceed with a common purpose.

It is generally assumed that it is part of the director's role to provide this stimulus and maintain it throughout the rehearsal period. Different directors use different means to accomplish this task. With some, it takes the form of constantly building up actors' confidence, whether justified or not, on the dubious assumption that confident actors will perform better than insecure ones. But viewed objectively, false confidence is a form of deception—or child psychology on (usually) discerning adults—and should be resisted. Any actor worth his salt knows when he is being pumped up with false confidence, just as he knows when his work is in trouble and in need of genuine help. The arguments against "false confidence" are manifold. Not only is it an insult to an actor's intelligence, but it is very likely to backfire when a production, buoyed up with unjustified praise, turns out to be a hopeless turkey. This utterly destroys a director's credibility and gives him the reputation of being either dishonest or stupid or both.

But a sense of communal identity collectively shared is an invaluable tool in drawing the best out of actors. Rehearsals *always* have a common purpose: the realization of a playwright's work by that particular confederation of artists. But it is more likely to be achieved through the palpable interaction of the actors involved than it is through being "handed down" from above by a wobbly or insecure director. When a director resorts to false confidence, it is an admission that true confidence is not possible, and since only true confidence can be truly beneficial, the aim of the exercise is defeated.

When a company of actors jointly perceives the meaning of a play and develops the artistic means of realizing it, a communal purpose organically arises. And how does this salutary state of affairs come about? It happens when actors discover individual truths that are collectively pursued out of a common quest to achieve shared objectives. Or to put it more simply: it happens when actors feel that the directions into which they are being led coincide with their own understanding of the material at hand; when the director's conception and the actor's conception *of* that conception are one and indivisible. When everything is making sense because there are no contradictions between what the actor is being asked to do and what he instinctively *wants* to be doing. When everything feels right, directorial suggestions are intuited by the actor before they are even given, and a director can honestly say: "I was just about to tell you to do that the moment before you did it."

In short, esprit de corps cannot be imposed from without. If it happens, it happens because there is an artistic continuity and an aesthetic harmony between all the members of the company.

Let's look at it from the other angle.

When an actor feels he is being asked to do something that his nature instinctively rejects, which goes against his understanding of both the role and the play, friction is inevitable. It may be overt or covert but it will be there, and if it is, harmony and confidence become impossible to achieve. That's when one runs up against those "artistic differences of opinion" that so often precede cast replacements, postponements, or cancellations: when some unquenchable virus has worked its way into the artistic process and corrupted everything with which it has come into contact. This is the opposite of esprit de corps, what one might call "contamination de corps."

True esprit de corps springs from artistic terrain being cultivated by artists who are in tune with one another. It cannot be grown in a hothouse and then transplanted into alien soil. But one also has to be wary of too great a sense of bonhomie.

It is pleasant to have warm social relations between all the members of a company, but it is not a requisite to good work. Often social harmony works against the objectivity that all rehearsals demand. After you become bosom buddies with your leading actors and regularly go out for a pint with them after every rehearsal, it will become harder and harder to criticize them openly, to expunge a misconception of a scene or a confusion about their characters' objectives. Meyerhold, a dictatorial director who was often insensitive to his actors and treated them merely as pawns in his "master plan," produced astounding results in the twenties and thirties in the Soviet Union. Stanislavsky often had very strained relations with the actors in the Moscow Arts Theatre. John Dexter was a monster to work with; Elia Kazan deliberately sowed feuds between his actors when he felt it would produce the effects he was after. In all these cases, esprit de corps was not a high priority.

One director I know put it this way:

> I am there to collaborate with an actor's talent, not to become their confessor, their lover, their drinking companion, or even their friend. When workmen are building a house together, they want to make sure the carpenters, the bricklayers, the plumbers, and the electricians really know their jobs so they can do theirs. I want equality of craftsmanship, not emotional ties.

The theatre is a place where temperament and conflict preside, where egos collide with egos, where tempers flare and strong feelings constantly well up and often erupt. But it is also a place where conflicts resolve and mutual affection flourishes. It is the Palace of Ambivalence. It always has been. It always will be. If you cannot come to terms with emotional contradictions of that sort, it is probably no place for you.

Rehearsing the Play

The word *rehearse* stems from the ancient French word *rehercier*, which originally meant "to harrow," which was an agrarian term that referred to breaking up or leveling soil with a farm tool called a harrow. It also meant "to inflict great distress or torment." Eventually, it took on its contemporary meaning, which is "to repeat" (*repetition* is the common French word for rehearsal) or "to recite aloud in a formal manner." It is curious the way many of these connotations still apply. Actors in the midst of strenuous rehearsals are often inflicted with great distress or torment; and of course, a rehearsal always involves a breaking up of the play into its respective parts; and if directors don't exactly use harrows to achieve their ends, they do frequently employ the whip.

The German word for rehearsal is *probe*—which means "trial or examination" and is in many ways a more accurate term. In creative rehearsals, material is "probed"—that is, tried out and examined, and in lackluster ones, words are simply repeated or recited aloud in a formal manner.

It is unfortunate that in most people's minds, rehearsing means repeating lines until they are learned by rote, as that can be one of the most deadening aspects of rehearsals. Of course lines must be learned, but as with all tuition, the *way* in which material is instilled into the mind is a crucial consideration. Learning by rote is destructive whether you are a schoolchild or a professional actor. Learning by rote is a form of self-hypnosis. It drills sounds into your brain but doesn't impress the meaning or significance of what is being embedded. If actors begin a memorization process before they have had a chance to discover the nuances of meaning contained in their roles, they succeed in conveying only text, forfeiting the subtext, and the former without the latter is utterly nonproductive.

An actor rehearsing with script in hand, trying only to "get his lines," falls into a self-mesmerizing state—a state in which contact with others is virtually impossible. His only real need in relation to his fellow actors is to be fed cues. It is *cues* that he anticipates and *cues* that he hears. Instead of experimenting with a variety of personal choices and responding to impulses relayed by others, he clings to the superficies of the play—the text—and is virtually imprisoned in its cocoon. His primary contact is not with other living beings or the inherent meaning of their speeches but with his own stressed-out powers of memorization. He is in a sense publicly "wanking," trying to work up personal experiences by acting *off* rather than *with* his fellow actors. A director would be well advised to douse such an actor with a bucket of cold water to try to bring him back into the collective fold.

Every rehearsal, like every character and every scene of a play, must have an objective, and it is sometimes useful for that objective to be publicly stated by the director. "Today, we are going to concentrate on the atmosphere needed in this scene." Or: "Today, we are going to see if we can generate the brisk rhythm demanded by this situation." Or: "Today, we are going to abandon all previous choices and adopt new ones, whether they work or not." Or, quite simply: "Today, we're going to play for the sake of unbroken continuity, to see if we all have our lines."

Actors immersed in creating roles have their own agendas, and sometimes these are at odds with the director's or those of their fellow actors. By announcing what the purpose of a rehearsal is, a collective objective is clearly established. One must always remember that a "company" is a set of disparate artists who are wholly enveloped in their own concerns, and it is the director's job to integrate them.

All rehearsals proceed on the basis of trial and error (mostly error). The most dangerous assumption of rehearsals is that everything one needs to know about the play has already been discovered and all that now remains is to refine and polish first impressions. That closes the door to a treasure trove of riches that could be discovered if the actors' attitude toward their work remained skeptical, tentative, and exploratory. In a healthy rehearsal session, an insight from one actor can suddenly become the compass-swing that sets everyone else off in a different direction. The great danger of rehearsals is that they often close down investigations (probes) before all the evidence of the text has been thoroughly tested. The actor's attitude toward the role must be like that of the explorer who, having found an estuary, immediately goes in search of the river. To assume that the literal meaning of a text is the equivalent of its subtext is to be misled into thinking that the trees *are* the forest.

Some directors say too much; some say too little. A director who meticulously describes the kind of reaction needed in a particular moment in the play might just as well mimic the desired reading. "Monkey see, monkey do" is too often the tactic used by lazy or ostentatious directors. Describing a character's reasoning behind a strong emotional moment may lead an actor to select a reaction that is pertinent to that description, but then it would be the result of the actor's choice, not the director's prompt. Long-winded lectures about the meaning of a scene or a particular action may so clog the actor's mind, open up so many contradictory possibilities, that he finds himself paralyzed (so many centipede legs that the centipede can no longer walk).

Giving actors preferred inflections is a waste of time. Unless an actor understands the intellectual process that produces a particular emphasis, the mimicked inflection will never take root. An *inflection*, after all, is a nuance of meaning that tilts a phrase in one direction or another. If the actor doesn't understand that nuance, it is virtually impossible for him to express it. No one can intelligently express what they don't understand. (Look at neophyte lecturers working from Cliffs Notes or drama critics writing about intellectually profound plays, the import of which has soared right over their heads.) The actor has three great tools: voice, body, and intellect, and the greatest of these is the intellect. And, it must be added, this is the one that the director must be most concerned with.

Many directors work from a blueprint: a tangible or conceptualized pattern of precisely what they want to see on the stage. They prescribe their moves on the margins of the script and draw little doodles to denote where, when, and how the actors should move. This is almost always disastrous. (I say "almost" because it is the way Max Reinhardt and Vsovolod Meyerhold worked, and they were two of the greatest directors of the twentieth century. But unless one is lucky enough to be a reincarnated Reinhardt or Meyerhold, it can be fatal.)

A play is a collective action conjured up over a prescribed period of time by a specific set of actors who invariably possess more originality and imagination than any single director can possibly muster. To ignore the wealth of creativity that is burgeoning in an acting ensemble is to discard the most powerful tool at the director's disposal. Once harnessed to the director's ideas, that tool is capable of more complexity and surprises than any director can possibly premeditate. It is the *interaction* of a company that produces solid artistic results, and it is the director's task to activate that interaction. To do this, one has to first provide something like a tabula rasa: a field that eventually becomes a "unified field." I deliberately included the qualifiers "something like" because there is a world of difference between a director with a vision of what he wants to produce and a director who, not having a clue, expects the company to provide one. A vision is something that that can be shared, and a shared vision can encourage actors to fill in a tabula rasa and thereby create a unified field. It is never a matter of bestowing total freedom, but rather freedom based on basic precepts elucidated or intuited by the director.

Peter Brook and Declan Mulholland are good examples of directors who create a free context that still operates within a prescribed frame of reference. There are hundreds more who, postulating total creative freedom, produce only aimless rubbish. The inescapable tension in all art is always between freedom and form. How much freedom? How much form? And the hardest thing in the theatre is getting the balance right.

Try as he might to bestow unbridled liberty, the director is always imposing form on his actors. His staging and set designs already circumscribe the spatial parameters of his actors, limiting where they can or cannot go. His urgings in the direction of character, situation, and intentionality further influence the free impulses of his company. Fidelity to the playwright's wishes as set out in his stage directions is another curb to the actor. Audience expectations, its mores and sensitivities, are built into both actors and director, and are also factors that dictate what choices will be made.

Convention and the irresistible lure of cliché—which is very much alive in all rehearsals—whittle things down even further. An actor often feels he has hit upon exactly the right note the moment he reproduces an intonation, an emphasis, or a gesture that other actors have effectively conveyed before him. Sometimes actors are too green to realize they are simply rehashing clichés; sometimes it is because a clichéd reaction has become second nature to them. The director's bullshit detector must always be turned on and scouring the work of the company. When it finds crap, it must bleep loudly.

When should a character stand up, sit down, cross the room, make a gesture, turn his head, wring his hands, square his shoulders, stamp his foot?

Who knows?

Presumably the playwright, who has created the character and therefore is aware of his mood swings and how they affect his body language. But then, every actor will feel these things differently depending on his own psychological make-up and his own interpretation of the play's language and events. There are innumerable ways of conveying feelings that express themselves corporeally. Shouldn't the director suggest them as he is "interpreting" the play—that is, realizing his vision of who these people are and how they interact with one another? Yes, but what if his notions run contrary to the impulses of the actor and the preconception of the playwright? What if an actor's way of expressing agitation is by suddenly beginning to do push-ups and a director's impulse is that he should begin chewing his fingernails? Either piece of business may convey the same point—as might any one of a dozen other actions.

The pattern of staging, specifics of stage business, proximities between characters, rises and sits, crosses and turns—in short, the whole of the characters' physical life on stage—is perhaps the hardest thing to ascertain, mainly because the impulses that motivate them are among the last things actors discover in their roles and yet the first things they are obliged to provide.

Discovering the true subtext of the play is a necessary first step in determining its proper choreography. Only when we are sure of what a character is feeling can we find actions that correspond to his inner state. But again, the actor will know this better than the director, for he is living constantly with his character, whereas the director has to concern himself with *everyone's* motivation. For that reason, the director should act as a kind of Geiger counter, examining every natural impulse that persuades an actor to approach, to withdraw, to sit, or to gesture. The "staging" is already forming in the instincts of the actor who has mastered his text, and a director is well advised to monitor, rather than impose, what he takes to be the proper pattern of movement.

That doesn't mean that he abdicates his responsibility to stage the play. His instincts, like those of the actor, are also germinating during the early stage of rehearsals, and when blocking begins, the actor is dutifully waiting for instructions from the director as to when and where to move. But sometimes his directions go against the actor's grain, and when that happens, the director is well advised to reconsider them. The actor's instincts regarding his character, being so much more deeply rooted than the director's, should be used as a guide to him, and he should be prepared to alter, or experiment with alternatives, as soon as the slightest resistance appears.

There is one school of thought that holds that the director gives the actor his moves and the actor's job is simply to *motivate* them—no matter how far-fetched they may be. But when they contradict the actor's deepest instincts, all the director is really doing is encouraging the ingenuity of the actor to make sense out of intractable material, to exercise his ability to resolve contradictions. A director must direct, but rather than "giving" directions, he must receive them from the play and the players. The best directors are wise enough to realize that a creative actor will come up with more pertinent material than he can ever invent himself and that his true job is to inspire creation rather than impose it.

A good deal of a director's time is spent evoking atmospheres relevant to his play. But in the course of his work, he may well encounter atmospheres generated in the rehearsal room that are the outgrowth of personal, rather than professional, tensions.

For instance, animosities between actors may stem from resentments of one sort or another, minor or major ego-kriegs due to one actor's theoretical orientation being at odds with another (e.g., Method actors vs. "old-fashioned technical actors") or simply clashes of personality between people who hail from different backgrounds and mores who simply "can't stand each other." Irrelevant as these conflicts may be to the work at hand, they nevertheless *affect* the work at hand, and it is the director who has to resolve them.

A problem of this kind occurred in a production I was staging in Edinburgh, in which one actor's animus against another took the form of violent physical attacks. The aggressor happened to be a large, muscular Welshman with a notoriously short fuse and his victim a short, puny young chap with no muscles to speak of. The cause of the attacks seemed to be nothing more than a loathing the larger man had developed for the other, provoked by the latter's habitual air of levity. The big guy, who was overly serious and something of a drinker, was provoked by the other man's frothy sense of humor to the point where he felt the need to whack him around.

In trying to reconcile these combatants, it was necessary to appeal to some cause greater than their mutual antagonism, and of course, that was the show. And once that was accepted by both parties, there was, if not a lasting truce, at least a cessation of hostilities. Everything—illness, aggression, paranoia, depression, lateness, fatigue, sloth—is subjugated to the almighty, all-embracing sovereignty of "the show." In the case of lesser conflicts, the same imperative needs to be invoked. It is the show that insists that differences be made up, hostilities dissipated, and quarrels reconciled.

The solution is really an ancient one. The god to which all Greek theatre genuflected was Dionysus, and it is useful to have a god presiding over the machinations of mortal actors, because there has to be a power higher than the producer's, the investors', or even the public's, and Dionysus beautifully fits the bill. So in times of turmoil, it is useful to remind artists that their petty squabbles must be dissolved for the sake of something higher than themselves: the play is not only "the thing" but an embodiment of the show, which of course "must go on." Whether the Dionysian spirit actually dissolves ill feeling depends on the eloquence with which directors invoke it, but it is a useful arbiter when arbitration is required and human referees prove inadequate.

In the last quarter of the rehearsal period, the director is obliged to begin stumble-throughs and then proper run-throughs. Too often, actors begin running through long before their exploratory work has been finished, and as a result, hatches are battened down far too early and fallacies or motiveless moments get fixed in stone. But at a certain point, the director is obliged to coagulate all he has done and judge the assembled continuity of his show. This is always a scary moment. When all the parts become one, certain omissions or misjudgments will immediately be noticed. At that point, it would be ruinous to continue "running through," as that will only solidify the rot. That's the point where one must return to the flawed segments and try to repair them, and only when they are fully repaired should run-throughs resume. The start of run-throughs is like the final stage in pottery when the vase is fired and then glazed.

When the performers are exposed to public previews, the director needs to relax his grip. The actors must be allowed to "breathe"—that is, freed from the restraint of the mise-en-scène, allowed to exercise their God-given "right to play" and in so doing test their choices through audience reaction. It is the first snip in the umbilical cord that connects the director to his company, and with each exposure to new audiences, that cord will be progressively frayed and ultimately severed—and that's exactly the way it should be. During rehearsals, there is no one more vital to artistic continuity than the director. Once the audience arrives, there is no one more dispensable.

"Remember this is Cleopatra, the sexiest and most desirable woman in Egypt, and you adore her. Now let's try again!"

Giving Notes

When a production reaches the run-through stage and the need to maintain unbroken continuity becomes essential, the director's way of making changes and improvements is through notes, usually given at the end of each run. The actors huddle around the director, who desperately tries to decipher the scribbles he has made and, by means of verbal corrections and suggestions, attempts to refine—and sometimes alter—the course his production has taken.

This ritual (and in many ways it *is* a ritual) reinforces the hierarchy that has always been taken for granted in the theatre. The director, a benevolent or terrifying authority figure and an audience of one, conveys to his company what he feels about the work that has thus far been accomplished, the goals achieved or unrealized, the missteps or peccadilloes he has noticed along the way. And in so doing, he reconfirms the authority that has been tacitly assumed but never openly declared: that is, that the actors have been giving form and feeling to his vision of the writer's work.

That is not to suggest that throughout rehearsals the actors have slavishly relinquished their own personal preconceptions of their roles, for in many instances, they have been tacitly clung to and, consciously or unconsciously, secreted into the emerging interpretation. But when the play reaches the run-through stage, any contradictions and misconceptions that may exist become glaring, and there is very little time to remove or rethink them. That is the point at which actors pay dearly for nurturing "private moments" whose motivation may be egotism rather than relevance, histrionics rather than plausibility. For at that stage, the arc of the play has become abundantly clear—both to the director and his company—and anything that veers away from that arc needs to be firmly expunged.

Most notes are technical in nature. "Rise here, rather than there"; "Cross right, rather than left"; "Stress this word, rather than the other"—but if they consist only of a litany of technical directions, they will be serving the production very poorly.

For it is in the final stages that the director should be revisiting the perceived story of his play, the underlying meaning of its developing situations and the unfolding meaning of its chronology. It is a time for rediscovering the production's earliest intentions and testing them against final results.

This is also the period when a director, like the headmaster he sometimes is, doles out rewards to his prize pupils, recognizing this one's humor or that one's agility, the marked improvement in this characterization or the radical transformation in another. It is also the director's last opportunity to correct missteps or vagueness and a time when he must be most politic. In private, he can be as unguarded as he likes to his actors, but in the communal atmosphere of the note session, it behooves him to use his utmost tact—for each actor is now comparing his performance with another's, and if publicly disparaged, there is danger of imposing a humiliation from which no constructive good can ever arise. On these occasions, it sometimes pays to be oblique. If you want to cool down an overheated performance by an actor who is prone to overacting, it may be useful to address your remarks to his playing partner about the degree of proper intensity the scene requires and, in passing, suggest a lowering of its temperature. The overheated actor will get the point even though the note is not directly addressed to him.

Some corrections can be made through notes; many cannot. If it's a matter of a wrong inflection or a slightly altered move, an apposite note can usually fix it. But if it's a piece of business between two or more performers, you would just be wasting your breath. Only finite, hands-on rehearsal can rectify such moments, and merely citing the problem verbally without scheduling the time to rehearse it is useless, as actors are being told something is wrong but not given the opportunity to put it right.

The note session imposes objectivity on a process that is enveloped in subjectivity. The actor's tendency throughout rehearsals has been to shape the logic of his role. This inevitably leads to self-absorption: the *actor's* lines, the *actor's* moves, the *actor's* motives, the *actor's* psychology. When notes are introduced into the process, the director who has been constantly insinuating his own preferences posits the first objective view of events the actors receive. It is as if a camera that has been shooting an endless series of close-ups suddenly dollies back to provide a comprehensive long shot of everyone's work. It is an essential and salutary change of focus, one that the actor needs in order to be able to evaluate his work in relation to everyone else's. That is why it is important for the director to speak in general terms as well as merely cherry-picking particular flaws or imprecisions. It is at this time that the actor is depending on his director to provide the larger view; that is what the audience will be seeing. If he doesn't provide that objectivity, if he clings to the correction of his precious minutiae, he is abdicating his true responsibility: to become the representative of a force greater than the writer or his company of actors—namely, the "public" for whom, ostensibly, all these efforts have been undertaken.

"One never knows when the RSC might call!"

Working with Egotists

Everyone has an ego, and in the theatre, egos come in three sizes: enormous, colossal, and humongous. This is just another way of saying that artists of every stripe have idealized conceptions of themselves, which is why they often produce both spectacular successes and monumental disasters.

An actress acquaintance of mine, who over the years had built up a prodigious reputation for herself on the American stage that included Tony nominations and a number of outstanding regional awards, found herself in her sixties auditioning for a television series in Hollywood. The interviewer was a bright young thing recently graduated from UCLA. Her first question was: "Could you tell me a little about what you've actually done on the stage?" The actress was a little dumbfounded but felt it politic not to reveal her surprise. She rattled off a number of top-drawer Broadway productions, many of which were opposite a roster of imposing male stars. The names of those productions meant nothing to the casting director, and even many of the celebrity names produced only blank blinks. It became clear that the generational gulf that yawned between the interviewer and the actress could never be bridged. As she left the casting director's office, the actress was in tears and seriously contemplated giving up the business.

To performers, the items on their résumés are a chronology of public achievement: creative experiences they have undergone at various stages in their lives that have turned them into the artists they have become. Their "credits" are, in a very real sense, the meaning of their lives: a catalogue of achievements and a validation of their worth. But to someone unfamiliar with their work, they are simply the names of anonymous plays, films, and TV roles, no different from those inscribed on the hundreds of résumés that land on agents' desks day after day. An actor's ego is an impenetrable citadel that contains real and imaginary triumphs, which, because they have been experienced by audiences and witnessed by professional observers, constitute an irrefutable monument to their reality. To deny *that* is to deny the very essence of their existence.

Every artist involved in the theatrical collaboration possesses, to some degree, a heightened sense of self. It cannot easily be set aside when questioned or assailed by a director. That is why a director needs delicacy and discretion when intruding on an actor's sense of his role, because in so doing, he may be invading a well-armored fortress that, as is to be expected, will be heavily defended.

At the beginning of a rehearsal period, all the scrutiny is on the text and the slowly evolving performances. Actors do not openly declare that they have a "heightened sense of self" or that they have an instinct about how their characterization should evolve. It all happens on a subconscious plane but is easily surmised in the actor's manner, inflections, and choices. The director divines the actor's conception of his role through minute hints and suggestions emanating from the actor's reading. Missteps or serious misconceptions must be detected as early as possible, because they are the bricks and mortar out of which the actor's interpretation will be constructed. If misguided or contrary to the director's understanding of the material, they need to be deracinated immediately, for if they are permitted to grow and take on girth, they will ultimately become impossible to uproot.

The tolerant, easygoing, unobtrusive director, who lets an actor's misconceptions develop even as he experiences uneasiness about their implications, will have no defense against the actor who, urged to rethink his characterization only days before an opening, complains: "Why didn't you say something three weeks ago if you thought I was going in the wrong direction? Why tell me now, a week before we have to go up?" In the face of such a rebuke, the tactful, polite, and unobtrusive director will not have a leg to stand on. It *was* his duty to raise a red flag the moment he sensed the actor was on the wrong track.

But let us assume the director *does* intercede early in the game—say, in the first week that actors are "on their feet," albeit with scripts in hand. What if the tentative actor resents directorial interference while he is at that delicate stage during which he is still testing the waters and experimenting with different options? He can justifiably complain that the director is choking off his oxygen, refusing to allow him to find *his* way, to flesh out *his* character and formulate his personal interpretation.

It is a legitimate conflict of interests. No actor wants his performance to be dictated by a director, and no director wants his conception of a play's meaning distorted or derailed by an interpretation that runs counter to what he wants his production to express.

According to protocol, the director should prevail and the actor fall in line. After all, an individual characterization is only a cog in a wheel that contains many spokes. But occasionally an actor's notion, though opposed to a director's pre-conception, will supplement or even improve the whole. Sometimes an alien idea effectively realized will bring an unexpected dimension to the proceedings whose repercussions will enhance all the surrounding performances. Sometimes, in short, an actor's instinct is superior to a director's, more inspired and more transformative.

It is in situations such as these that ego most threatens the collective effort. For the director's insistence on *his* way may be nothing more than a deep-seated resistance to having his authority put into question. By the same token, the actor may feel that his artistic integrity is being violated when asked to surrender to the commands of a director who will not bend to a fresh idea that he did not originate.

Egoistic confrontations of this kind are almost never resolved openly. The actor suppresses his resistance, the director suppresses his indignation, and the company suppresses its inclination to take sides. A contretemps of that kind often can sour the rehearsal atmosphere irreparably.

As I have said elsewhere, a useful temporary solution is for the director to encourage the actor fully to demonstrate his new insight so that everyone, the director included, can gage its efficacy. If it is subsequently rejected, at least the actor has the satisfaction of having given it full vent before an impartial jury—that is, the company. But if it turns out to be a fructifying idea—one that excites and appeals to others, an idea that causes each member of the company to alter or adjust his performance to the betterment of the whole—the director may have unwittingly been presented with an invaluable gift, a hidden insight that refertilizes the material and enhances its power. If that is not the case, if the actor's idea is off the wall and fundamentally wrong-headed, it will ring false to everyone in the rehearsal room, since all actors are umbilically connected to the context from which every new idea springs.

So incursions of ego are not to be treated as a nuisance—a manifestation of the actor's irrepress-

ible desire to "show off" or "hog the spotlight"—
but possibly as a lucky strike that owes its discovery to the reflections of an actor who has turned the tedium of a routine, scheduled flight into a rollicking journey on a magic carpet.

I am referring here to ideas that are relevant to the realization of a playwright's work: always a delicate maneuver fraught with dangers. There are other, more traditional ego problems that concern billing, press coverage, placement in curtain calls, the size of one's dressing room, the color or accessories of one's costume, the length of one's bio in the program, the degree of illumination on stage commensurate with one's conception of one's reputation—all of which are, at base, childish quibbles that should be treated by the director in the following manner: a straight line should be formed by the entire company, all of whom should be issued a baseball bat. The offending actor should be forced to stand with his back to his fellow players and forced to repeat the words "I am an insufferable ham and contemptible human being" at least two hundred times. That done, each actor should take turns whacking the offender firmly on the backside until sitting comfortably is no longer an option. If desired, this ritual can be accompanied by boos, catcalls, whistles, and cacophonic music, which may give it a somewhat greater sense of humiliation.

Friendly Advice

During rehearsals and particularly during previews, actors will discover that there is a legion of friends and acquaintances beyond the precincts of the theatre offering advice on their performances. Let's face it. Everyone who attends the theatre is an armchair critic; after all, they all buy tickets that entitle them to an "armchair," and so it is easy to fall into the delusion.

Occasionally, if these friends and acquaintances are extraordinarily astute, they can come up with an idea that has not occurred to the director, the playwright, the designers, or others in the company. But more often than not, they are a conglomeration of kibitzers with no discernible critical faculties who enjoy the frisson of being involved, no matter how peripherally, with the formulation of theatrical art. They often persuade themselves that they are assisting their thespian friends by providing helpful and objective reactions from "average spectators," which, if acted upon, may smooth over some of the rough spots of the gathering production. After all, everyone is entitled to an opinion, aren't they? Well no, they aren't! Some people are more entitled than others—such as critics, directors, producers, and play doctors. Just as one wouldn't consult the greengrocer about questions of nuclear fission or brain surgery, so it makes little sense to approach people with no direct knowledge or experience of theatrical art on the finer points of play production.

In Stuttgart, I was directing an adaptation of *Taming of the Shrew* in which Katherine was depicted as an embittered termagant who not only hates men but despises both her father and her sister, Bianca. The object of the production was to bring out the cruel and vindictive side of Kate and jettison all the broad comedy with which this play is usually overloaded. Although this was made abundantly clear to the company at the outset, as rehearsals progressed, I found my Kate incorporating comic business: doing "takes" and even mugging. I assumed this was some kind of necessary release from the rigors of living with the grim and unrelenting Katherine that we had been assembling from the start, a psychological need on the part of the actress to relax a remorselessly negative characterization.

After rehearsals, she would scoot off with the dramaturge, a young man with whom she appeared to have created a strong personal liaison. It soon became clear that the dramaturge, convinced that this was one of Shakespeare's merriest comedies, was infiltrating ideas intended to lighten and brighten moments that I was intent on making as dark and cruel as possible. When confronted with the subversion, the actress admitted that she was trying to make Katherine simultaneously harsh and comic. I pointed out that the two simply didn't mix and that unless we reverted to the original conception, she would have to be replaced. That seemed to persuade her to proceed along the given lines, and ultimately, the former Katherine made a triumphant return. (The dramaturge, meanwhile, was barred from rehearsals and given a tongue-lashing more severe than anything Petruchio ever bestows upon Katherine.)

During rehearsals, a variety of impulses and intentions develop in members of the cast, and for the most part, these are healthy responses to the work being insinuated by the director. But occasionally, an idea develops that is not only at odds with a director's interpretation but positively violates its aim. These alien notions usually stem from close friends or acquaintances who find that a performer's work contradicts their conception of a familiar play or one they cherish for qualities that are no longer apparent. The more radical a director's interpretation, the more actors will balk at fulfilling it—unless the earliest discussions have clarified the direction a director is intending to take.

The director must understand that he is collaborating not only with the physical presence of actors but with their world view, philosophy of life, and deeply embedded sense of values. That is why, to revert to what has been said earlier, it is essential that the director guide not only the external geography of the production but its inner network of ideas as well. If you can sell your vision of the play to your actors, then everyone is in the same coach headed in the same direction. If you neglect that essential part of the job, you will find the course of rehearsals filled with quicksand and booby traps. A director, you will discover, cannot impose a geography on the play unless he has first elucidated the philosophy that informs it. The only exception to that rule is with those hardened, anti-intellectual actors who insist they want only to be given their lines and their moves and offer themselves as putty in a director's hands. Some directors prefer such actors above all others, but putty usually hardens into cement, whereas human beings with open minds remain resilient throughout.

"He's always been a great believer in Method realism."

Let There Be Light! (But in Moderation)

When theatre first began, it played by the light of day. It then went indoors and played by candlelight, then gaslight, and at the end of the nineteenth century, electricity. The object was always the same: to enable members of an audience to see the actors do their stuff.

When electricity became computerized during the twentieth century—controllable, sophisticated, capable of immense subtlety and transformations—lighting took on a life of its own. It was as capable of being shaped and colored as set decoration, and so it acquired "designers." It could be harnessed to an ingenious mechanism called a *light board*, which could not only be turned on and off but could blend colors, project lasers, and create moods and movement of its own. It acquired almost as much versatility as actors, and eventually it would produce light shows that dispensed with live actors altogether.

In the midst of all these astonishing refinements, its main aim was still to light the action, but because directors and lighting designers were eager to demonstrate all the myriad effects it could produce, more and more lights were added and more and more light effects incorporated into productions. Instead of simply being switched on and off, lights performed according to a "light plot"— just as actors performed according to the play's plot. Today, in cities such as Paris, Las Vegas, Tokyo, and New York, lighting has become a kind of showcase for astounding technological ingenuity, and the lighting designer has become a major player along with the set and costume designers. And perhaps that is the trouble. Because lighting has become so remarkably versatile and so readily available, the theatre cannot resist utilizing it in a thousand different ways.

All this is an elaborate way of suggesting that perhaps lighting has become overused in the contemporary theatre, often doing what *actors* should be doing and frequently doing the same thing that they *are* doing—not so much gilding as overilluminating the lily.

Lighting can certainly create atmosphere, but before there was lighting, actors generated atmosphere by themselves. A mood, atmosphere, or emotional state *can* be augmented with lights, but in many instances, these effects need no augmentation whatsoever. Actors produce them using their voices, their bodies, their imaginations, and their ability to convey feeling.

In the case of musicals, thrillers, science fiction, Grand Guignol, or plays charged with distinctive atmospheres, lighting is often an invaluable tool. But in ancient classics or anything written between the fifteenth and eighteenth centuries, the function of lighting is essentially to "light the language"—which simply means generating enough illumination to make the actor's words as clear as possible. Lighting effects frequently immerse the stage in shadows or cascades of colored light, which, attractive as they may be, reduce the intensity and the clarity of what actors are actually saying.

Lighting designers, whose conceit can sometimes rival that of celebrity actors, are forever looking to "express" themselves within the context of a production, bursting with suggestions as to how to enhance the proceedings. But often their contributions only draw attention to atmospheric and emotional changes that are already happening between actors. A good lighting plot is one that is virtually imperceptible to an audience; a bad lighting plot is like an extra character that has somehow wormed its way onto the stage and is shadowing actors wherever they go: unwanted, unnecessary, and uncalled for.

Lighting should be an illustration of the director's conception of his production, not a compromise worked out between a director and an eager lighting designer. Long before the show reaches that final stage where the lighting designer is called in to watch a run-through, the director should have sat down with the script and marked out where he wants specific light effects, where "specials" are required, where levels should be increased or diminished, what the overall tonality of the lighting ought to be. These instructions must be conveyed to the lighting designer in the same way the director has conveyed his general notion of the play to his set designer, and of course he must insure that the set designer and the lighting designer act in tandem, as the work of one is inextricable from the work of the other.

Once the director has passed on his instructions, the lighting designer has received his brief and the next step is to employ his ingenuity and expertise in realizing those directions. But often, that is the point where the lighting designer seizes opportunities to "express" himself—to embellish what has been asked for and concoct brilliant additions to what the director has prescribed. That is the moment when lighting produces redundancy and the lily begins to get gilded.

"The secret of life," said Louis Jouvet, "is timing." It is certainly the secret of lighting. The length of a fade-up or the abruptness of a blackout is part of the "punctuation" I spoke of earlier, and it is as important with lighting as it is with writing. Directors trying to calculate the length of a fade-out to achieve the maximum dramatic effect may spend an hour experimenting with precisely what that timing should be. A slow fade of ten seconds sends a completely different message from a fade-out of three seconds or a snap-blackout. Sometimes one is required; sometimes the other. If the gap between scenes is too long, it produces an uncomfortable rustling among the audience. There is a kind of tendon that connects the end of one scene to the next, and if it stretches too far, it can break.

If a scene change exceeds two minutes, the illusion that has been progressively worked up may be dispelled. If it goes on much longer, it will certainly be broken, and that is a difficult spell to recapture. Nobody gets up and stomps out of the theatre; nevertheless, the damage is done. Work lights, used while stagehands set up the following scene, if too bright may seriously impair a play's continuity. The timing *between* scenes is as important as the timing *within* scenes. If an intermission goes longer than twenty minutes, something in the next act suffers as a result of the longeur. It is almost imperceptible, but it is there. The audience's suspension of disbelief is made of thin mesh; almost anything can shred it. One has to ask: What degree of "suspension" is possible? How long can people wait expectantly to see what will happen next, and at what point, because the gap is excessive, does an audience metaphorically wash its hands of the whole business?

When God said, "Let there be light" and "saw that it was good," He very sensibly installed a fade-up and a fade-out, dividing "the light from the darkness." Despite the nuances with which He endowed dawns and sunsets, starshine and moonshine, He worked from a fairly simple lighting plot. It would behoove modern designers to do the same.

"I've taken the liberty of making a few
judicious cuts in your script."

They Also Serve Who Stand and Wait

Is there any job more frustrating than that of the understudy: eyed suspiciously by the lead actors whom they furtively shadow, hammering in lines and moves they may never perform, hoping against hope that some calamity will befall their assigned actor so that they may finally be allowed to step out of the shadows and shine?

I exaggerate of course. They are not really scheming villains out of *All About Eve*, and they do not all seethe with envy and frustration, but still it is a thankless task, and consequently no one thanks them for it. But they are essential safeguards in productions, and the director must insure that, like the sprinkler system, they are in a constant state of readiness.

During rehearsals when "beats" are first being decided and motives unraveled, it is difficult to split one's attention between leading actors and those that may be asked one day to take their place. The director simply assumes that the understudy, who attends all the rehearsals of the actor he is covering, will be imbibing everything that is happening. During those laborious weeks, the stage manager has usually called some understudy rehearsals to insure that the "covers" are completely versed on any and all changes taking place in the production, but understudies almost never get the benefit of first-hand, up-close-and-intimate directorial interpretation—which they should.

If understudies simply ape the actors whose roles they are covering, they never bring a personal dimension to their work, and that is a debit where one could have a credit. Before rehearsals reach their frantic final stages, the director is well advised to spend a few hours with the understudies so that they can hear the tenor of their own voices and obtain personal insights into key scenes. It is in the understudy's nature simply to copy what others are doing, but often that doesn't capture the spirit or flavor of the material. The understudy has a personality and sensitivity of his own, and if he is going to be thrust into a performance at short notice, it makes sense to have awakened those unique traits in regard to the role he will have to perform at short notice.

Obviously, the overall interpretation remains the same, and it can be disastrous if understudies are permitted to bring new, untested choices to their roles. An irresistible temptation among some understudies is to outshine the actors they are covering, especially if it's an opening night or a special performance with VIPs in attendance. Occasionally, an actor who is genuinely gifted can pull something astonishing out of the hat that bears almost no resemblance to what the original actor has established. That happens a lot in backstage movie-musicals of the thirties and forties, but in reality, a clever but untried interpretation impulsively flung onto the stage can be ruinous to a production in which all other performers have meticulously assembled their parts in relation to a prearranged whole. One way of avoiding disagreeable surprises like that is to insure that the understudies' own personalities have been adapted to the needs of their characters, and in order to do that, the director—and not just the stage manager—is obliged to rehearse them.

The practice of allowing understudies to take over certain performances (i.e., matinees or less populous nights of the week) is a healthy one, as it gives them an opportunity to test their readiness before live audiences, and so if necessity suddenly

forces them on stage, they are not entirely discom-
bobulated. Actors' Equity, in its restrictive wis-
dom, frowns upon the practice, and so understudies have to endure the shock of being thrown in at
the deep end—sometimes at a point in the run
when understudy rehearsals have been discontin-
ued or allowed to become slack and remote.

What is needed, of course, is a complete over-
haul of the system, so that the floating crew of
understudies is regularly utilized at certain inter-
vals during the run and all the labor expended in
preparing for a role is not stillborn in them. The
more they are permitted to share in performances,
the more they will have some degree of personal
fulfillment.

The understudy definitely fits Milton's
description of those "who also serve" although
they "only stand and wait." But the prompter is
also an unsung worker in the theatre and, again,
one whose role is a vital cog in the creative process.

When actors are "off book" but not yet firm in
their lines, they rely on the prompter to stabilize
them. In continental theatres, the prompter or *sou-
fleuse* is a distinctive member of the company

whose value is clearly appreciated. In American and English companies, it is usually an assistant stage manager who "holds the book" during rehearsals and occasionally doubles as prompter during performances. Someone has to do it, and the ASM seems the logical choice, but since it is not considered a professional task in its own right, it is very often a makeshift operation.

In European rehearsals, the prompter frequently whispers the text along with the actor mouthing it. This practice would drive American actors out of their squeaking little minds, as they are accustomed merely to calling for cues as they need them, but continental actors seem to rely on the custom and are inured to it.

There is an art to being an efficient prompter, and it's not one that is taught in either drama schools or college training programs. When an actor is struggling for his next line, the first few words are often enough to enable him to recall the entire speech, and a good prompter provides only these. A bad prompter either doesn't provide enough words or supplies too many, irritating the actor who simply needed a reminder, not a full-fledged recitation.

A good prompter anticipates the telling pause in an actor's speech and knows that it is his cue to supply a few key words. A bad prompter mistakes a dramatic pause for a "dry" and sends the actor ballistic by throwing in the next line when he knows it perfectly well and is taking his own sweet time to get to it.

A good prompter can tell the difference between a character's hesitation and an actor's struggle for the next word. A bad prompter sometimes preempts the actor by anticipating a dry when none is there. A good prompter accepts the outbursts and impatience that an actor displays as being part of the process of mastering his role; a bad prompter takes umbrage and receives the actor's indignation as a personal affront, defensively pleading: "I was only trying to help!"

The reason a prompter is a vital part of the rehearsal process is because he is the custodian of its continuity. By simply filling in the gap in an actor's memorization, he permits the gist of a speech to consolidate itself in the actor's mind. By interrupting the actor's struggling consciousness with too much or too little of a prompt, he impedes the actor's attempt to bridge one phrase to another and, consequently, to lodge it in his brain. It is up to the director to lay down the rules for prompting—to insist on short, abbreviated prompts rather than long, awkward ones; to insist that dramatic pauses be clearly written into the script so that the prompter doesn't mistake them for dries; to know when a prompt is sufficient for an actor to continue on his own; and to prompt only *words*, not intonations, inflections, or alternative readings.

Some prompters feel they must whisper the sought-for lines, but in most cases this causes added aggravation to the actor who cannot hear them. A good prompter should speak loud and clear when giving prompts in rehearsals, softly and just-about-audibly during performances. But these gradations need to be drummed into their heads by directors, who must develop an instinct as to what helps or hinders actors trying to master their text.

The prompter can become a terror in rehearsals: a goad drawing public attention to the fact the actors do not know their lines. He can become a pariah in a company because of the delicate job he performs. But so long as prompting is

treated as an informal kind of assistance by anyone who happens to be free to hold the book—and
not a discipline in its own right—it will impede
rather than improve the actor's art.

Public Relations and the Photo Call

It may seem irrelevant to advise a director about the conduct of something as mundane as a photo call, but the fact is anything that affects the well-being of his actors must be of concern to the director, and a photo call is a procedure that engages the egos of his whole company, projects an image of the play to the outside world, and is a factor that can affect the morale of the entire cast.

A photo call usually takes the form of an invitation to the press, prior to the opening, to come and take pictures of the actors in their makeup and costumes for distribution to media outlets, and it is common for the director to suggest the scenes or "setups" from which the pictures will be taken. It is also something of a mini-premiere, for extracts from the production are, for the first time, being presented to outsiders.

If you have a cast of ten but only two name performers, it makes good sense not to invite the remaining eight actors to the call. The photographers will only be concerned with the celebrity actors, and the others will be ignored. If, however, the cast members are equal in reputation, it is essential that all are called and photographed in their respective scenes. The cameras legitimize the existence of the actors and the bond that unites them—that is, the play, the production. I have been to many photo calls where after hours of fastidious preparation with costume and makeup, only two or three actors have actually had their pictures taken. The actor's ego responds powerfully to such slights, and that kind of neglect creates bad blood among the entire company.

The photo call should be treated as a mini-performance. The actors should be introduced to the photographers; some words about the play, its style and its purport, should be dispensed. Although photographers are always eager to obtain "action shots"—broad gestures and moments of visual (often violent) excitement—the director should urge them to consider portraits and simple two-shots, especially if the play is a drama or has quiet or intense moments. The photos should attempt to capture the spirit of the piece and not simply startling poses that may have no direct bearing on the character of the play. The director should direct the photo call as carefully as he would the curtain call, adjusting positions as may be necessary to get the most out of the camera but not "posing" shots that have no bearing on the play or its intentions.

Usually, only a small number of these photos will appear in the press; sometimes none. But having their picture taken awakens the deepest sense of self among actors, peaks their vanity, and projects an outward image of a highly complex inner state. It is a ceremony and should be treated with caution, respect, and sensitivity.

In many professional productions, the photo call has been replaced by photos taken by a staff photographer, who is permitted to shoot at will during a dress rehearsal. Often, these shots capture the brio of a live performance and are preferable to any setups a director may devise. But in my experience, photographers, even house photographers, prefer to set up pictures in carefully controlled conditions so that they don't have to try desperately to keep up with the pace of a live performance: seeing a great shot but missing it because it flies by too quickly. Good theatre photographers are as special as gifted set or lighting designers and should be given their heads.

A production begins a long time before the first day of rehearsal. It actually starts when an announcement of the show appears on an editor's desk. The press release is the harbinger of the play and its production. It is what creates the first impression of the work about to be undertaken. If you are working on a serious domestic drama and the press release suggests it is a rip-roaring comedy along the lines of Neil Simon or Georges Feydeau, that first impression will be warped and generate misunderstandings. Therefore, a director should always insist on approving everything sent out to the press that refers to his production. It is *his* language, rather than a publicist's, that should convey the gist of what is being readied for public viewing. No more than fifty or sixty well-chosen words should encapsulate the story; there may be a few words about the style or the origin of the work. Most of it should deal with biographical information about the actors and the collaborators. It is far too early in the game for anyone, even a director, to speak authoritatively about what will be concocted during a five- or six-week rehearsal period, and if you say too much too soon, you may regret your rashness.

Publicity, press releases, photos, and all preliminary information released to the public about something that as yet is not even a work-in-progress creates an expectation. It is like being greeted by a stranger: what he says and how he comports himself constitutes a first impression, and as we all know, first impressions can be positive or negative, endearing or disastrous.

"She has to upstage everything—even the
goddamn curtain call!"

Take a Bow

Actors are obsessive about curtain calls, and if a director is not sensitive to this obsession, it may be his undoing. In the catalogue of professional manias, curtain calls are second only to billing.

It is the director's job to organize the call in such a way that it properly reflects the hierarchy of the company. But that is not always easy to ascertain. The supporting roles are clearly identifiable, but when you get to the leads, things tend to get murky. If, for instance, you have a high-visibility actress in the role of Lady Macbeth and a less experienced one in the role of Macbeth, which should be given prominence in the curtain call? Most directors would agree that the former takes priority over the latter, despite the fact that Macbeth is the larger and more dominating role. But if you have a tetchy actor playing Macbeth, his subordination in the curtain call may cause resentment. If you give both performers a joint curtain call, the more accomplished actress may feel she is not being given her due. It sometimes pays to discuss the sequence of calls with the actors in advance of the curtain-call rehearsal to feel them out on what you (and they) believe is the correct order.

Calls are frequently arranged in doubles—or, in the case of larger casts, quartets: two or four actors coming out simultaneously. This gets your company on stage in an expedient manner and reduces the length of curtain calls, which can often be tiring to audiences that feel bludgeoned into protracted applause when all they really want to do is gather up their coats and avoid the inevitable traffic jams. But leading players expect that they will be given a solo curtain call, and clearly, if you are presenting Hamlet or Lear, Tartuffe or Tamburlaine, Hedda or Medea, they are fully entitled to it. But what if you are presenting an all-star version of *The Importance of Being Ernest* and your Lady Bracknell is a celebrated character actress and your Cecily and Gwendolyn are well-known TV personalities? Should one persist in believing that Jack and Algernon are really the leads and that therefore they should appear last?

The simple solution to pecking-order problems of that sort is to bring the principals out all together, half from one side of the stage and half from the other: to have an ensemble call. Let each artist individually step forward for his solo call and then gather them all up again for a final group call. If, as everyone claims, theatre is a collaborative art, collective curtain calls make the most sense.

These may seem to be infantile quibbles, but they are not perceived as such by the players. The hierarchy of curtain calls has a significance for them that directors do not always grasp. It is their time with the public or, as they perceive it, *their* public, and in regard to the performance of that play on that night, they are absolutely right. It is *their* interaction with the spectators that constitutes the show, and it is only proper that at the final curtain, the two parties most directly involved in the evening's events should commune.

Sometimes, an actor who has been enthusiastically received by the audience is coupled with a weak actor who has left virtually no impression whatsoever. The fact that they share a curtain call together is subversive to the more popular artist. ("If I weren't standing beside this galoot, they'd be cheering their heads off.") Or contrariwise, the duller actor finds himself the subject of an ovation that is clearly intended for his partner. He is, of course, delighted, but his partner, who is the real cause of the furor, has fumes flaring out of his nostrils. Invariably, the unimpressive actor will tell his fellow artists: "Did you hear the cheers they gave me at the curtain call?" and unless they are particularly spiteful, they will assume a fixed smile and allow their benighted companion to live on happily in Cloud Cuckooland.

In a production of Ionesco's *Makbett* in Coventry, my cast included Harry H. Corbett, who had become a popular favorite in the series *Stepney and Son*, and Terry Scott, a popular TV personality in his own right—both of almost equal standing as British comedians. Corbett automatically assumed he was the star of the show and behaved accordingly. At the end of those performances where audience reaction was particularly warm, he would step forward from the curtain-call lineup and, blithely assuming the leadership of the ensemble, make a little speech on behalf of the cast. Scott, frozen in the line behind him, would seethe quietly and go purple in the face. His speech completed, Corbett would smile his goofy, ineffectual smile and step back for a final round of applause, assuming everyone loved and adored him as much as he did himself. I don't believe Scott's anger ever erupted, but had it done so, it would have demolished the theatre and a good deal of the surrounding neighborhood.

Curtain calls are mini-dramas in themselves and immensely varied. Some, particularly in musicals, merge unobtrusively into the final scene. Some reveal subtle human factors that inadvertently convey themselves to the audience.

Sometimes at a curtain call, the manic glaze in actors' eyes suggest a perverse joy, as if the sound of smacking palms were the equivalent of orgiastic flagellation. Sometimes, as in Russia, the actors clap back as if the audience's contribution was not a whit less than the performers'. In continental companies, the unrehearsed actors often mill around, bumping into each other, and peer back stupidly at the clamor exploding around them. Some actors give their best performances at the curtain call. Donald Wolfit used to lean against the proscenium arch, clutching the curtain like an exhausted gladiator, implying that no public burst of energy—no matter how vigorous—could equal the labors he had just undergone.

Some actors don a mask of jolly complicity, their expressions insisting: "We all did it together." Some actors, many of the best in fact, go rigid with tension or receive their volleys of applause like so many dollops of castor oil. Still others turn down the sides of their mouths and contemptuously bide their time, considering the plaudits of the mob to be a wholly unjustified intrusion into their craft. Some, the more egoistic, wallow in the sound as if it were music from the spheres, fantasizing personal triumphs by mentally transforming dull thuds of polite applause into Vesuvian eruptions. Some stand around, jitteringly contemplating the trains they will catch and the late dinners they will shortly wolf down. Some actors, at the end of a long, satisfying performance, step forward like the triumphant torero to receive the ears of the prize bull. Sometimes, in certain political productions, the curtain call is a massed act of defiance with actors radiating their antipathy to a disgruntled and disgusted public, and one can hear the crunch of conflicting ideologies crackling through the auditorium.

There is one curtain call I have never forgotten.

It came at the end of the National Theatre production of Carl Zuckmayer's *Captain of Kopenick*, which starred Paul Scofield. The actor's gaunt, creased, tousled head peered into the auditorium, clutching the hands of his fellow actors as if permitting the public to view his genius, untrammeled by art, undisguised by artifice. Then, stepping forward to the apron, he gave the kind of gracious nod that King George probably threw to Handel when he stood up in his box during the "Hallelujah Chorus" of the *Messiah*. Then, being waved forward by his colleagues for a solo call, he forged silent bonds of brotherhood with the audience, bowing to acknowledge—and at the same time confirm—the mastery of his craft and the perspicacity of our appreciation of it. Then he smiled wanly, as if to say: "Life is not all art and you would be wise to temper your enthusiasms with a certain amount of philosophic detachment." He held out his hands again to invite his fellow players into a charmed circle, and they approached him tentatively, as if he were a witch doctor too charged and holy to touch, but they touched nevertheless: grasping his hands on either side and receiving the magic electricity that the house had authorized him to distribute evenly among his colleagues. Then, waving his hand wanly as one might to a departing train, he shuffled down to the privacy of his dressing room while our applause evaporated in the air like a kind of aimless obstreperousness that, having made its point, had outlived its usefulness.

I can't for the life of me remember anything about the play, but the curtain call is enshrined in my mental archives.

Maintaining Discipline

Once a play opens, it has a natural tendency to go to pot. The director's vigilant eye is removed, actors begin experimenting with new readings and new business, moments that in rehearsal went "just so far" suddenly go to extreme lengths, and the nightly presence of the audience tends to encourage overplaying and gaucherie. The success of a performance is now gauged by how many new laughs can be eked out of the public, without reference to their relevance or suitability. In worst-case scenarios, the actors behave like children whose adult supervisors, having left the premises, allow their basest and most unruly instincts to run riot. Where the director was a strict taskmaster, their new authority figure—the audience—is almost totally permissive, and actors, again like children, take full advantage of their newfound liberty.

There is one school of thought that holds that the true performance of a play happens only when

the director leaves the scene and actors enter into
a new and spontaneous relationship with the public. There is an element of truth in that supposition, as actors need to be allowed to breathe, and a
strict mise-en-scène can be like a tight corset,
restricting rather than containing their natural
instincts. But in a properly maintained rehearsal
process, the director and his cast have already
experimented with various calibrations of feelings.
They have tried going "over the top" in certain situations and, having discovered that moderation
often pays greater dividends, were accordingly
pulled back. A proper rehearsal process has, in
fact, established precisely what the maximal
expression of a playwright's work—and a director's interpretation of it—should be, and usually
there has been unanimity about those determina-
tions. To discard all those carefully arrived-at decisions, to ignore all those laborious experiments
and the precious insights they wrought, is to vio-
late the integrity of the entire theatrical process. It
is to say, in effect: None of all that mattered; what
really matters is only what we "get back" in terms
of audience reaction. It implies that the discrimi-
nation of the artist is in some sense inferior to the
appetites of his audience; that the artist is there
only to satisfy the needs of his public, to give the
audience "what it wants."

But we know full well that the audience is a large, undifferentiated blob, whose character changes from night to night and who, if asked, could not even begin to articulate what it wanted because, in a philosophic sense, there is no "it" and thus no way of expressing its true "wants." If members were polled, their replies would be like that of the Philistine who doesn't understand art but "knows what he likes." The fact is they want to be moved to laughter or to tears; they want intellectual stimulation; they want to be transported and transformed. They want satori and a sense of euphoria. They want what great art, artfully crafted, occasionally delivers, but apart from wooly generalizations of that sort, they cannot *explain* what they want, and it is pointless to turn to them for guidance.

Theoretically, the artist *does* know what he wants or at least what he is after in any given work. That is the premise behind all theatrical endeavors: to find a correlation between what a work means to artists and discovering the means of conveying that understanding to others using the tools of their trade. That is why audiences buy tickets and celebrate artists: to be given something they themselves cannot produce. It is fatuous to ask to be tutored by those who openly confess they haven't a clue as to how these things come about. And when actors take their cues from audiences instead of relying on their own instincts and imagination, they are reversing the natural process by which art is created and the public edified.

And so it is essential to preserve the results of what one has diligently assembled through strenuous creative effort over the length of the run. This can be monitored by having an assistant director who keeps tabs on the performances as they unfold, or by relying on the nightly reports of an attentive stage manager, who should be encouraged to note down all deviations from the agreed-upon mise-en-scène. If permutations begin to appear, re-rehearsal is permitted under most union contracts and should be rigorously undertaken. No painter once his canvas had been hung up for exhibition would allow the exhibitors to tamper with his work, and no director should permit a company's natural exuberance or inspired second guesses to alter the shape and design of the production he has diligently assembled. Quite apart from it being a violation of theatrical etiquette, it often puts the director in the position of having to defend embarrassing choices he never approved but which are inevitably attributed to him.

During the run of Joe Orton's *Loot* in London's West End, I returned to my production after an absence of several weeks to find the lead actor performing the broadest kind of baggy-pants, red-nosed farce. When I challenged him on the excesses of his performance, his defense was: "I'm getting more laughs than ever before," without taking into account that the nature of those laughs violated the playwright's subtleties and removed the darkness that made that play a black comedy. My ream of new notes and strictures about excess didn't go down well either with him or his fellow actors, but they were vigorously enforced and, fortunately, seconded by the producers.

A similar fate befell *What The Butler Saw* at the Union Square Dinner Theatre in Las Vegas, where I watched a sophisticated comedy filled with witty wordplay and contemporary satire played like a lascivious, down-and-dirty sex comedy. It is sometimes inconceivable to actors that there are moments in a play where *one doesn't want a laugh*; where, in fact, a laugh is a violation of a playwright's intent and an offense against his style. It is in circumstances such as these that the actor can rightly be said to be "whoring for effect": a weakness that besets all actors and is particularly rife among those trapped in a long run.

"I dunno, I'd say it was a sort of mixed review."

Surviving the Reviews

In the life of every show, there comes a Day of Judgment: the day the reviews appear. For actors and directors, this can be a traumatic time. After all, most theatre artists are generously endowed with egos—or they wouldn't be in this profession to begin with—and egos are as fragile as aspic.

Almost every show opens with a gush of optimism, an eagerness to present the public with the fruits of its artistic labor, and in nine cases out of ten, the product is judged to be wanting. People who have delved deeply and worked industriously to perfect their art are obliged to confront the harsh realization that where they thought there would be magic, there are yawns; where they thought there would be laughter, there are fidgets; where they anticipated approbation, they have met with disdain.

Essentially, there are three kinds of reviews: the Out-and-Out Rave; the Irritated Dismissal; and the Mixed-Bag Notice, where virtues and vices are matched against one another to create a kind of critical mishmash that, for both performers and readers, conveys no clear-cut impression whatsoever. The latter is the most problematic. Often the gist of the "mixed notice" is something like: "The acting was rotten, the play is a dud, the production stinks to high heaven, but the sets were gorgeous." Performers translating this review to their friends say something like: "The settings received raves, but other things were somewhat qualified." When both actors and play have been resolutely panned, the automatic response is always: "But the *audience* loved it," which, when one thinks about it, has to be an unverifiable speculation, because audiences do not write reviews, always applaud at curtain calls, and almost never express displeasure until they have left the theatre. If you are lucky enough to get a violently obstreperous negative reaction, spurned by one and all, the show will fall mercifully into the category of "controversial," and ironically, that often saves your bacon.

What, then, is a constructive way of responding to reviews, be they either raves or pans?

A discerning critic can open a window on a show that neither the director nor the actor ever knew existed. The light that pours through that window can elucidate factors that, never previously noticed, can usher in an entirely new perspective. A cogent review suddenly illuminates the work of artists, and that illumination, if taken to heart, can conceivably be used to remedy or improve the remainder of the run. If nothing else, the criticism—assuming it is lucid, perceptive, and honest—bestows a genuine intellectual satisfaction. With the precious gift of hindsight, one realizes what one has done, where one has failed or succeeded, what the nature of the beast really is. Given the degree of effort and dedication invested in every stage production, that is a boon of a kind.

But what if the review is fatuous, misguided, obtuse, and has simply missed the point of the entire exercise? Should one meekly accept fallacious responses only because they appear in the public prints? Obviously, that is insupportable.

I believe a director and a company know when they have legitimately failed. Something in their psyches gets confirmed by the bad reviews, and the public's verdict, rather than generating hostility, is tacitly accepted. But given the inferior level of most theatre reviews (and the fact that there usually aren't enough of them for good ones to counter the bad), it is perfectly legitimate for off-base criticism to be vigorously rejected. When that happens, it is the audience that becomes the show's tutor, and actors learn from their reaction what works or doesn't work.

Here, the attitude of the director is crucial. If he caves in because of bad notices, he is as useless to his company as he is to himself. But if he can discriminate between sensible criticism and fatuous journalese, he can insinuate a number of subtle (sometimes radical) changes in the production that to some extent may remedy its failings. Should this occur, word of mouth can sometimes counteract negative reviews. People who have enjoyed the performances become advocates for the show and antagonists of the reviewers. It is generally agreed that if the public is antipathetic to a show, even glowing notices will not enable it to run. It is equally true that if they are supportive, a show can survive mixed notices and dramatically turn itself around. *Abie's Irish Rose*, which enjoyed one of the longest runs on Broadway, was savaged by most critics when it opened. More recently, *I'm Not Rappaport* resurfaced despite negative notices, and there are innumerable examples of miraculous resurrections among musicals.

The artists' attitude toward reviewers should be civil—even though the critic's attitude toward them rarely is. The premise here is that the critic is part of the theatrical pyramid, albeit perched on the apex and with the sharpest point. Critics are first and foremost journalists, but their obligation to produce readable copy is sometimes at odds with their ability to cogently analyze the goods before them. They are also in the difficult position, from which playgoers are free, of articulating precisely what they felt about what they saw, and as anyone who has ever written criticism for a living will tell you, that is an excruciating obligation. This is mainly because feelings generated by plays do not come in single blocks but in waves: I like this, I don't like that; this is plausible, that is not; etc., etc., ad infinitum. The critic has to integrate all these contradictory feelings into a coherent opinion. The sound critics realize that a so-called objective or balanced review is simply a form of equivocation, because neither artists nor the public want a scorecard of the evening but rather a general evaluation that comes down clearly on one side or the other. It is possible to draw a fair critical conclusion about an evening's entertainment without burdening the reader with the literary equivalent of a mess of pottage—possible, but not easy.

Criticism is inescapable in the theatre. The director is, as it were, the critic of the production, and every rehearsal consists of instructions that inherently "criticize" what an actor is doing and how it's being done. The playwright is subject to criticism from the director, the dramaturge, and the producer. He is constantly being urged to cut and change, modify, or strengthen his work. Tacitly, actors are criticizing the style of the director, the deportment of their fellow players, the validity of certain rewrites or deletions. All theatrical art is carried on in an atmosphere of intense analysis and evaluation. Taste is constantly being assessed; efficacy tested. The drama critic is the terminus of all these critical efforts: certainly not the last word, but one that can contribute creatively to the end product.

Working with the Playwright

When directing a play by a living author (who is usually granted the right to attend rehearsals), the director will find himself in an awkward position. The power base is suddenly split. Surely, the director is the captain of the ship and his word is law. And yet, here is the author, without whom there would be no "words" at all—so to which authority should the actor be beholden?

If the playwright has the stature of someone like David Mamet, Harold Pinter, or Tom Stoppard, the author's influence is often paramount, and there are frequent consultations between director and playwright, the contents of which do not seep out to the company except as directives previously agreed upon between both parties. However, if you are working with a new playwright, you might consider an alternative arrangement that may prove more effective.

The first thing to realize is that many fledgling playwrights do not understand the process by which a play gravitates to the stage: that a variety of people with creative talents—that is, actors, designers, dramaturges, and so forth—are reshaping the original material in the act of interpreting it. Sometimes this may alter the playwright's original vision, and sensible playwrights realize this is *sometimes* to the good. But there are some playwrights who find it difficult, if not impossible, to relinquish the picture of the play they have in their minds, who insist on tangibly reproducing those images that first arose in their imaginations. I am not implying that a mise-en-scène should transform the nature or spirit of the original work, only that the act of interpretation opens doors to other people's conceptions of what a playwright has created, and unless the writer recognizes that he is moving from one genre into another, and one that has its own special requirements, he will come unstuck.

The playwright should be in attendance during the two or three reading-rehearsals in which the actors are seated around the table with scripts in hand. He should be pumped for as much information as he can possibly give, and everyone concerned with the production should have a chance to bombard him with questions. Once he has been pumped dry and the actors get on their feet, he should be prohibited from attending rehearsals. This may sound draconian, but it is a practical measure. Once actors have begun struggling with their lines and formulating their moves, they become sorely inhibited if the playwright is present. They are not sure whether or not he realizes that those early, tentative, necessarily imperfect efforts are part of the process of looking for and finding the route into the play, and they are painfully conscious of the fact that everything is in disarray—the *inevitable* disarray that precedes the decisive choices that will shortly be made.

Once the play is ready for its first runthroughs, the playwright should be invited back to see the work in its embryonic state. At that juncture, he will have an idea of which way the material is moving, and if he has strong objections, that is the time to voice them—to the director, of course, not the actors. That is the same point at which the director will get an objective impression of what has already been created. The playwright's absence during the bulk of the rehearsals has given him an invaluable objectivity that he could not possibly have had otherwise. His reactions at that stage will be extremely pertinent, and it behooves the director to give them very serious consideration. Often that is the moment when the playwright himself decides to alter and revise, delete, or re-angle. It is also the point when the director has an opportunity to ventilate the problems he has encountered with the script. It is the second plateau of the rehearsal period, where the production is not quite off the drawing board, but *almost.*

Once the impressions of both director and playwright have been honestly evaluated, it is possible to visualize what the shape of the final product will be. The freshness of perspective for both parties provides a great opportunity to seriously assess the fruits of their joint labor. Once this has been accomplished, the remaining run-throughs and previews should attempt to assimilate these new insights.

During that last stanza of the production, the playwright's criticism should be relayed exclusively to the director—never directly to the actors. Nothing subverts the authority of a director more than suddenly discovering that actors are responding to the playwright's notes rather than his own. This is not a matter of bruised egos. It is simply that the playwright has neither the language nor the technical expertise to remedy the problems that have emerged, and just as the director would not have the audacity to revise the playwright's lines, so the playwright should not interfere with the communication that has been assiduously built up between the director and his company. A playwright may be able to tell an actor succinctly what is wrong with his performance, but usually he hasn't the vocabulary or theatrical background to know how to correct it. In short, the chain of command that initiated the production process should not suddenly be subverted, as that tends to disconcert actors, upset directors, and be fatally counterproductive to the playwright's own remedial intentions.

When I was directing a triad of plays by Murray Schisgal in London (the first professional productions, in fact, of this writer's work), the author would stalk up and down the aisle at the back of the theatre, wringing his hands and mumbling his dissatisfaction with the actors' work—so much so that the actors complained to me that they couldn't possibly rehearse freely knowing that the playwright was being so chagrined by their efforts. I explained this to the author and, to safeguard the morale of the company, banned him from daily rehearsals until the production was ready to open. This was very early in Mr. Schisgal's career, and no doubt he thought it very high-handed of me to bar the playwright from his own play, but my choice was a simple one. Either the playwright remained and the actors became progressively more distressed or the playwright went and proper work could be resumed. I had no hesitation in making my decision.

Recently, there was a production of a play in California that I knew from the start was seriously overwritten and badly in need of editing. I also knew that the playwright in question was very anal retentive about his material, as I had had a previous experience with him during which I felt obliged to forsake the production because of his unwillingness to make changes or deletions. To avoid a reprise of that unhappy situation, I entered into a written agreement with him that (a) he would accept whatever cuts the company and I would make in rehearsal, and (b) after the first readings, he would leave the scene, to return only when run-throughs were in progress. Reluctantly, the playwright accepted those terms. During rehearsals in which we proceeded to trim the fat from the script, I found myself having to protect the play from the excessive mayhem the actors were anxious to inflict upon it. The result, I can report, was gratifying to both the author and the public. But that was a unique situation. Usually, one commences rehearsals with a script already pared down to essentials. In this case, it was a play with obvious excesses clearly in need of editing, which needed to be carefully assessed before cuts were made. It sometimes happens that there is a slender work of art entombed in a flabby exterior (like Cyril Connolly's belief that "imprisoned in every fat man, a thin one is wildly signaling to be let out.") That was exactly the case here.

Working with a playwright who has chosen you to direct his play is sometimes like being invited to a sumptuous feast on the condition that you don't spoil the table setting by actually eating anything. Or it can be a marvelous tête-à-tête between two kindred spirits who clearly relish the same delicacies.

Curtain Speech

There is a certain cycle that a director goes through when he directs a play. At least I do. I can't swear that it applies to all directors, but it may.

In the lead-up to rehearsals, there is a great welter of ideas percolating in one's brainpan and a bubbling enthusiasm to get started. Once the cast is assembled and rehearsals have begun, the initial burst of enthusiasm subsides and is followed by a sense of resignation in regard to the cast (which always involves a compromise of some sort) and a total preoccupation with the minutiae of the production. By the middle of rehearsals, everything looks wrong, and you wonder how you could ever have got into such a hopeless mess. You contemplate both postponement and cancellation and, in extreme cases, giving up theatre altogether and becoming a supermarket bagger. This depression lasts until the final stage of production, when necessity takes over and you have learned to settle for less—at which time, if you are lucky, you experience a great energy surge similar to the one that galvanized you in the first place.

All stage productions are exercises in compromise. I suppose you could say everything in life is something of a compromise, and the pain of compromise is always commensurate with the degree of idealism that has had to be sacrificed. Most people in the theatre start out with an enormous amount of optimism, an irrepressible zeal, and the highest of hopes (which is perhaps why so many people working in the profession become manic depressives). That maelstrom of expectation that first possesses you confers a very intoxicating high, and so naturally when you plummet down to earth, you land with a resounding thud.

Directors, like most people, have to make choices between preference and necessity. Some people do shows because they are burning with a desire that cannot be quenched. If they were offered no compensation whatsoever, they would still channel all their energies into the work and nothing would deter them from realizing it. Others accept assignments for a number of more prosaic reasons: because it is the best that is "on offer," the money is good, or there is a certain prestige involved in working with celebrity actors and it is therefore a smart career move.

Because idealism is always tempered by necessity, it would be foolish to suggest that a director should only tackle a project when he is brimming over with enthusiasm. (There are many instances in which a director agrees to undertake what appears to be a dry or pedestrian project and gradually discovers it stirs an excitement that he never anticipated.) But generally speaking, there is a correlation between the director's eagerness to undertake a particular show and its final result. Being tuned into a piece of material, feeling there is some statement being made that is personal to you and that you wholly believe in, activates certain buds of invention that do not appear when a show is "just a job." Because of that correlation, a director should think very deeply about where he is going to invest the next four or five months of his life. (With preliminary meetings, strategy sessions, casting, pre-production planning, and post-performance monitoring, plays usually exact *at least* that amount of time.) The worst experience a director can have stems from accepting an assignment that every fiber of his body instinctively rejects. The reasons for acceptance can always be persuasively rationalized, but if you are going to spend a month or so trying to discern the hidden motivations of fictional characters, you should be astute enough to discover your own before signing a contract.

After he has completed a production, the director is not only entitled to a vacation, it is essential for his creative health that he take one. I don't mean six months on the Riviera or a cruise around the world, but enough time to recover from the onslaught of the last show. And it *is* an onslaught, because the director, as much as the leading actor or overworked stage manager, has expended an enormous amount of energy, and his exhaustion is, if anything, greater than the actors', whose batteries get regularly recharged each night as they step before a live audience. A director, on the other hand, can only look back with resignation or regrets on things he would have liked to play out differently: scenes that never quite worked or design choices that were never quite what they should have been but that are now unalterable. Ironically, this niggling, critical assessment preoccupies the directors of even highly successful shows that have been praised by critics, applauded by the public, broken box-office records, and won Tonys. It is as if true perfection can never truly be achieved in theatrical endeavor—perhaps because one is working with mutable human elements: actors whose performances are endlessly variable and audiences that are maddeningly unpredictable.

Being more prone to see the hole than the doughnut, I feel I may have overemphasized the negative aspects of this profession, so let me conclude by saying this:

There are moments during a performance when a certain other-earthly atmosphere descends upon the stage: a felt harmony between the effects a director has attempted and an actor has succeeded in realizing before a huddle of people quietly breathing in unison in a darkened space. This makes one suddenly believe the hokum about *magic* that the theatre is constantly propagandizing in its advertisements. When that happens, one is reminded of the theatre's holiest origins and its astonishing transformative powers, its ability to change people's lives. *Catharsis* is no longer a cold, academic Aristotelian term to be bandied about by academics. It becomes a palpable sensation that everyone gathered together in that encircling magical space experiences simultaneously.

In the final moment of a production of *Hamlet* in Gothenburg, after all the corpses have been removed, a battle-weary Fortinbras sits down on a stool. He removes his boot and turns it upside down, and a sprinkle of fine-grain sand dribbles onto the ground as the lights slowly fade. The moment contains both the futility of life and its unquenchable persistence. Nothing, neither war nor treachery nor decimated princes "that might have grown full straight," can impede its continuum. It is a moment that captures nothingness but at the same time celebrates everything. And it is moments like these that make directors feel that every frustration, every betrayal, every calamity the theatre can come up with, is worthwhile.

When actors, no longer in remote rehearsal rooms, are in the final stages of run-through in the auditorium of the theatre in which they will be performing, the stage manager sets up what is referred to as a "God mike" so that the director's voice can be heard clearly throughout the house. A director is someone who plays at being God. He calls the tune, sets the goals, and raises or lowers the bar, according to his whims or his talent. Despite harsh strictures and often peremptory manners, he is always a benevolent God, because he is in the business of creating universes—which is what every new play production is.

It is a privileged position, and most directors understand that. It permits them to transform ideas into tangible forms, using sentient human beings who, in most cases, accept their authority and give them what they want. This is not an ego trip (although in worst-case scenarios it can be) but a promise made to a company of actors that something new and wonderful is going to be collectively created. An experience that has never existed before is going to be cobbled together with planks and passions, notions and conjectures, trials and errors.

The buzz of a first day's rehearsal is the buzz of dedicated men and women perpetuating the traditions begun by Aeschylus and Sophocles, Marlowe and Shakespeare. Theatre began as a holy ceremony; it remains so to this day, and the director is its high priest, shaman, and miracle maker. The director and his human building blocks—the playwrights, actors, and designers—are engrossed in one of the most essential activities human beings can perform: demystifying the mysteries of life, elucidating its contradictions, recreating its finest and most appalling moments—trying to make sense out of the very same enigmas to which scholars and philosophers have devoted their lives since the dawn of civilization. Theatre provides logic and absurdity, empathy and commiseration, pleasure and edification—and sometimes life-altering transformation.

Who would not be elated to work happily and well in such a profession?